POV Press Publishing
Books by Bethanne Kim

Survival Skills for All Ages
>   *#1: 26 Basic Life Skills*
>   *#2: 52+ Recipes for Everyday & Emergencies*
>   *#3: 26 Mental and Urban Life Skills*

Scouting in the Deep End:
>   *#1: Cubmastering: Getting Started as Cubmaster*
>   *#2: Scout Leader: An Introduction to Boy Scouts*
>   *#3: Citizenship in the World: Teaching the Merit Badge*

Not the Zombies
>   *#1: OMG!*
>   *#2: BRB!*
>   *#3: YOLO!*

The Constitution: It's the OS for the US

The Organized Wedding: Planning Everything from Your Engagement to Your Marriage

Forthcoming:

Survival Skills for All Ages:
>   *26 Outdoor Life Skills*

Special Needs Prepping Scouting in the Deep End:
>   *#4: Mentoring Youth in Scouts*

SURVIVAL SKILLS FOR ALL AGES #1

26 Basic Life Skills

BETHANNE KIM

TWO CRAZY BOYS PUBLISHING

The cover art for this is part of The Jon B. Lovelace Collection of California Photographs in Carol M. Highsmith's America Project, Library of Congress, Prints and Photographs Division.

If you would like to support the work being done by Ms. Highsmith, artwork is available for purchase at:
http://photographs-america.hostedbywebstore.com/

eBook ISBN: 978-1-942533-17-7
Paperback ISBN: 978-1-942533-16-0

1. Reference – Survival & Disaster Preparedness
2. Parenting

Distributed by POV Press
PO Box 399
Catharpin, VA 20143

Printed in the United States of America

TABLE OF CONTENTS

NOTE: Please do your own research on any skill, product or advice before trying, buying, or relying on it, especially in an emergency. While the author has personally used certain of the products that are discussed (or similar products) in this series, she has not necessarily used all of the products, and some information is included based on third party recommendations, rather than personal experience. Nothing in this book is intended to, nor should it be used to, replace applicable medical or other expert or professional advice.

As of the publication date, all links are to information believed appropriate to this book. Due to the nature of the internet and third party control of links/linked information, there is no guarantee that links, or information they reference, has not changed since publication, or will not change in the future. If you find broken, erroneous, or inappropriate links or information, please email the author at theWiseMom@WiseFathers.com. **The author is not responsible for linked online content, information, advice, or products.**

ACKNOWLEDGMENTS

If it hadn't been for Lisa Bedford, The Survival Mom, I would never have had the idea to write this book and the rest of the series, including Everyday Recipes for Emergencies, Mental and Urban Life Skills, Special Needs Prepping, and Outdoor Life Skills.

One of the challenges all writers face is getting a great cover. My thanks to Kim Hill for her help creating the cover.

Of course, if it wasn't for my own two crazy boys, I wouldn't have had the experience to know what I needed to write!

So, my most sincere and deepest thanks to Lisa Bedford, my two crazy boys, and my ever-supportive and beloved husband.

Introduction

As parents, our most basic job is making sure our kids survive. Nothing else we can teach you really matters if you don't survive. But what do you need to know to survive and thrive? That is a complex question with a lot of possible answers

This book and two forthcoming ones–*26 Urban and Mental Life Skills* and *26 Outdoor Life Skills*–are all about the skills needed to survive and thrive, whether you're a kid or an adult.

The idea for these books came from a series of three posts I wrote for TheSurvivalMom.com that expanded on her very popular post "32 Survival Skills Your Child Should Know." But those posts are only lists! This series of books covers the material to get started on each skill.

At the end of each chapter, there is an activity and a five question Quick Quiz to help make sure you really understand the topic. Each Quiz is followed by a Resources list since these books only have space to introduce the topics. The Resources will help you really dive into the ones that grab your interest.

The Books and Other sections under Resources include links to products you can buy. I don't profit from those. It can be time-consuming to research items, so I added links to items I feel confident are good quality. Some I own, some I have used, some I simply researched.

But the Resources section is far from just about products! Some skills, such as knife sharpening, are hard to learn without seeing them. That's where the <u>Videos</u> come in. Admittedly, a few of the videos are just plain fun. Seeing seeds germinate isn't necessary to understanding sprouting, but it is darn cool.

Finally, there are <u>Scouting Specific</u> links for most sections. These links go to requirements for badges from both Boy Scouts and Girls Scouts. Even if your family isn't active in Scouting, those organizations have spent a lot of time and money creating age-appropriate activities to learn new skills. They are every bit as great a learning resource for non-Scouts as they are for Scouts.

As of 2015, Boy Scout Merit Badges are far more specific than the Girl Scout ones. The BSA Camping Merit Badge requires 20 nights of camping. The GSUSA Camping Badge says "head out on your trip–and have some nighttime fun!" This isn't saying one is better than the other, simply that one tends to have more detailed requirements.

One book cannot cover all the information on any survival or emergency related topic. That's why the <u>Resources</u> section is there: to guide the reader to websites, articles, books, and videos with more indepth information. The ones that seem the absolute best are marked with an *.

BASIC SURVIVAL

Hopefully this book helps you become more self-sufficient.

As a life-long Scout, my motto in life really is:

Be Prepared!

Bethanne Kim

{Part 1}
Basic Survival

Survival teaching often focuses too much on outdoor skills like fishing and purifying water. As great as they are, there are other basic skills that are often overlooked, some of which are even more critical to survival. That's what this section focuses on.

Trust your instincts. The truth is, kids are often told, in so very many ways, not to trust their instincts until finally, they don't. Once you stop trusting your own instincts, reversing that can be very hard, even as an adult.

No one deliberately tells another person not to trust their instincts, but every time you are forced to greet someone you don't trust, it chips away just a tiny bit more of your instincts about who to trust, and instincts can be critical to surviving in a true disaster.

Know who to trust. Even as an adult, it can be hard to know who to trust. For kids, it's even harder because adults often force you—with the best of intentions—to give a lot of trust to people you either don't know at all or barely know. You are expected to trust teachers from the first day of school, without knowing them at all. Scout leaders, youth pastors, coaches, and other adults all also expect a fair amount of trust immediately, without having done anything more than volunteer to earn it. Are they worthy? Perhaps–or perhaps not.

They will also tell you not to trust people they don't know or they don't trust, even if you do know them and they have established trust with you. Most adults have school friends their parents didn't like or trust but whom they trusted and liked. Their friends showed them something their parents never saw.

Know that there will be times your parents and the other adults in your life have enough life experience to see things you do not. There will be times they are right and you are wrong, but there will be times you are right and they are wrong. Try to be wise enough to listen to what they tell you, but don't lose trust in yourself.

Develop your situational awareness. We are all guilty of it to some degree. Our focus is on our tablet, book, conversation, or whatever and we have no idea what is happening around us. "Situational awareness" simply means being aware of what is going on around you so you can respond appropriately.

People who are situationally aware are less likely to be targeted for random crimes, like mugging, and more likely to leave the area before other crimes happen. (Small clues can warn them things are "off," causing them to vacate the area.)

Problem Solving. The very first step in problem solving is figuring out what your problem is. It is virtually impossible to solve a problem if you don't correctly identify the cause. Handling the aftermath of an EMP (Electro-Magnetic Pulse) would be very different than handling a power outage caused by falling trees.

Like most things, the more you practice, the better you get. Learning problem solving and practicing it in everyday situations will help you solve problems more effectively in an emergency situation.

Plan ahead. It sounds easy, but doing it routinely isn't always easy. Letting things slide and rushing around at the last minute to do whatever (science project, eat breakfast, pack for vacation) is more the norm. But rushing around often leads to forgetting things and making mistakes, and there isn't enough time to correct things if you haven't planned ahead.

Laying out clothing and making sure everything is ready to go for the morning is one form of planning ahead. Saving money for college, a car, a new tablet, or even a video game is also planning ahead. Planning ahead takes so many forms it is impossible to name them all. But whatever the form, planning ahead makes life go a little bit smoother and usually allows enough time to go back and fix anything you missed or did wrong.

Dress for the weather. No matter how good you are at survival skills, if it's now -4°F with wind-chill and you are dressed for 40°F, you are in trouble. Some parts of this are obvious. Most people know which coat and gloves they wear when it is cool, cold, or very cold, for example. But there are ways to be more dress more effectively for the weather. Layering is the prime example. If you do this well, your body will stay warm but you can adjust to fluctuations in both the outside temperature and your body temperature (exercise heats humans up) by adding and removing layers.

Be physically fit. Hopefully this is fairly self-evident, but if you need to hike a distance or squeeze through a small space to get to safety, being physically fit is critical. There are so many ways to get fit that everyone can find *something* they enjoy. Even an 80+ year old virtual-hermit I know exercises along with a TV show!

Exercising is also a great way to build muscle memory for skills you may need in an emergency. If you may need to bike ride or hike to get to safety in an emergency, spend some leisure time on those activities. Take the paths you would need and really learn them so you are comfortable riding/hiking them even if it's dark, wet, or slippery. In an emergency, that could make life a lot easier for you and those with you.

{One}

Trust Your Instincts

This is first because it is the most important thing: **No matter what your age, you need to recognize and trust your instincts.** Parents can't always follow, or possibly understand, what their kids tell them, but knowing what your instincts are telling you and explaining that to your parents is important.

As a little baby, your instincts tell you to stay with Mommy and Daddy pretty much every instant of your life. That makes sense because babies can't defend themselves, so of course we feel a need to be with bigger people who can do it for us.

As we grow into toddlers, some kids feel safe going up to virtually anyone, but most feel at least some stranger anxiety. Some are very shy and hide behind someone they know and trust rather than even show their faces to a stranger. Since we can't hide behind Mommy and Daddy forever, at some point adults start dragging us out and making us greet these other people, no matter how we feel about the matter.

It's hard because sometimes people just don't wanna, no matter how old or young they are. It's not a "stranger danger" feeling or anything like that, they just don't wanna, and parents really can't just go along with that all the time. Part of a parent's job is helping their kids, especially shy ones, learn how to interact with others, including strangers.

> **Note to Parents:** Parents know our own children. If your child is acting out of character, it's OK to humor them and ask later (in private) what happened. If they just didn't feel like it, talk to them so they know that next time they will be expected to shake hands, say hi, dance a jig, or whatever was asked of them, within reason.

> But if their answer shows that their gut was screaming "stranger danger" for some reason, let them know that's OK and maybe even that you are proud of them for noticing what their body was saying.

Recognize Your Instincts

I lost track of how many times my son complained in the morning that he didn't want to school because they were going to have a fire drill (never announced in advance) and they did, in fact, have a fire drill that day. At this point, if he said he was sure "something bad" was going to happen at school, I would keep him home that day.

It is a *very* rare person to be that certain of their instincts, or that accurate. I have no idea how he knew. Most likely, there was some pattern his subconscious noted of how the principal or vice-principal behaved or a weather pattern that tipped him off. (They do them once or twice a month in nice weather; if it had been rainy all month and it was a nice day near the end of the month, it would be logical to expect a fire drill.)

For most of us, unlike my son, our instincts are a quiet little voice we need to learn to listen to. Whenever your instincts do kick in, don't ignore them. Take a minute to think about how you recognized them and what they were telling you. After years of ignoring their instincts, many people don't notice their body sending messages until they begin getting headaches or stomachaches as a result of too much stress. Stress can be caused by ignoring our instincts.

If I am doing something I shouldn't, I start feeling very frustrated all the time, even when everything is seemingly going well, and then I start getting angry very easily. This is a clear sign (for me) that I need to change what I am doing. This usually happens because I ignore my instincts about what I *should* be doing and am instead doing what I *think* I should be doing instead of what I *feel* I should be doing.

Whatever it is that happens to you, make a note of it, maybe even in a notebook, to see if there is a pattern. Over time, as you become more and more aware of your instincts, the signals will probably get more subtle because you will notice them more quickly. I knew—simply *knew*—when I saw an email about a meeting that I needed to attend, so I did. Attending set me on a path to help others in my community that would have been more difficult and time-consuming to reach if I hadn't trusted my instincts.

CHAPTER ONE

Practice

Listen to the little voice in your head. It can be very, very quiet, or so loud you feel like someone is screaming inside your head. **Your inner voice almost always starts out whispering, so if it's screaming, it's probably important.**

Most of the time, it tells us small things that don't make sense, like "put the library book in the outside pocket" instead of the big pocket of your backpack. If you don't and your water bottle leaks all over the inside of your backpack later that day, you'll know why. Your subconscious may have noticed the bottle wasn't sealed the whole way, or the way that specific bottle always leaks. If you just do what that voice says, you may never know why.

Our instincts are often responding to small clues our subconscious notices that our conscious does not. The subconscious simply has better situational awareness (Chapter 3).

Our instincts are a good guide, but that doesn't mean they are always right. Our instincts, brains, experiences, and more work together to form our PGS (Personal Guidance System). Like a GPS, it helps us navigate our way through life.

Sometimes when we use a GPS, it suddenly tells us there is traffic ahead and re-routes. Sometimes, it chooses a route that we know isn't the fastest. And most annoyingly, it is all too easy to find roads that are right in front of us that the GPS doesn't know exist. And of course, sometimes they just plain break and we can't use them at all. None of this makes the GPS wrong or bad, it just means that we need to know where we are going, too.

In the same way, our PGS can give us bad directions, but it can also recognize dangers we don't see ahead of us and redirect us. If we ignore that little voice saying "recalculating" in our head, we may end up stalled in traffic or at a dead-end.

At the same time, you may know something it doesn't. A GPS never knows when a school is about to dismiss or a movie let out and the roads near there will become clogged. It also doesn't know which ones become an icy, dangerous mess as soon as little snow falls.

We need to rely on our brains as well as our instincts. If your gut is saying "cross that creek here and we'll get to help faster" but your brain looks at the rain-swollen creek and knows you will probably drown, go with your brain. That's what it's there for. Your gut may be right that it's closer to the creek, but it isn't seeing all the factors.

Think About Why

I have a heck of a time trusting one of my kids' principals. The man has done nothing wrong, but he looks like someone I had a bad experience with in the past. Recognizing why my gut is responding negatively to him helps me sort through how I should respond to certain situations.

Fear

Sometimes, the "why" is a fear so deeply ingrained in our subconscious that all we know is that we are afraid. I have a life-long fear of deep water for no discernible reason. I find it quite annoying, but conquering something with no cause is very difficult. Not impossible, but much more difficult.

The best way to work on conquering a deeply ingrained fear is by pushing the boundaries in smaller ways that are easier handle. Over time, even deep fears can become manageable in this way, even if they don't go away entirely.

With my fear of water, I started by dunking myself under so my whole head was under water. Then I dunked myself so I sat (briefly) on the bottom of the pool with a lot more water over my head. I also learned to swim properly both on the surface and under water so that I became used to having my face submerged for longer periods of time. Unless I tell them, most people would never know that I have a fear of water because I have taken baby steps that were not over-whelming to make it manageable. But I still avoid water slides.

It's important to remember that an emergency is *not* the time to over-ride your instincts about what you can and can't handle. Even if you are initially OK, it's all too easy to freeze up when faced with a fear and mid-emergency is a really bad time for that to happen.

Activity

Think about how you felt when you met your best friend or someone else that you trust. If you have had more than one, think about your favorite one first, and repeat it if you want. What else makes you feel that way? Was it like the first day of summer vacation? Or picking out a treat at the grocery store? Does it remind you of how you felt when you made something you were really proud of? Did they remind you of someone else you already knew?

Either write down how you felt or talk about it with your parents.

Now think about how you felt when you met someone you don't trust or like. It could be the annoying kid in your class or the bully on the bus. How did that make you feel? Was it like being yelled at when you knew you hadn't done anything wrong?

How do the two compare?

Those feelings may have been your instincts telling you this person was a good/bad person to have in your life. Next time you meet someone and you have similar feelings, what will that tell you about your relationship with them?

> **Remember:** Your gut is a good guide but, like a GPS, it isn't always right. Sometimes your gut tells you to trust/not trust a person because they look, sound, or act like someone you already know, but they are not that person.

Quick Quiz

T/F   Your gut is always right.

T/F   You should listen to your gut.

T/F   Your gut warns you about your personal limits.

T/F   Your gut never reacts based on past experiences.

T/F   Rely on your gut and nothing else in an emergency.

Resources:

Articles

*Can I Develop My Intuition?
http://www.takingcharge.csh.umn.edu/explore-healing-practices/intuition-healthcare/can-i-develop-my-intuition

Children's Intuition: A Special Key to Success in Life
http://www.naturalawakeningsmag.com/Natural-Awakenings/September-2009/Children-rsquos-Intuition/

Children's Intuition and Relaxation: The Direct Correlation
http://kidsrelaxation.com/uncategorized/childrens-intuition-and-relaxation-the-direct-correlation/

How to Follow Your Intuition
http://www.wikihow.com/Follow-Your-Intuition

Books

Body Language, Intuition & Leadership! Surviving Primary School (An inspirational children's books ages 9-12) by Dr. Orly Katz
Protecting the Gift: Keeping Children and Teenagers Safe (and Parents Sane) by Gavin de Becker

Videos

How to Keep Kids Safe Through Intuition- Gavin de Becker, Author & Security Expert
https://www.youtube.com/watch?v=plzyPXbsHp4

Kid on Wire: Let Children Take Risks and Learn to Trust Their Own Intuition, with Philippe Petit
https://www.youtube.com/watch?v=i7RGw_Smw8g

{Two}

Who to Trust

This goes hand in hand with trusting your instincts, and it can be hard. **Sometimes trusting too little can cost as much as not trusting enough.**

When we trust others, they have private information about us. If we are talking about strangers online, that information might be as simple as our real address and birthday. It could be schools we attended and our full name. Whatever it is, it's information that we don't want everyone to have. It is information predators, thieves, and bad guys can use to do Bad Things.

When we're talking about friends, it might be our deepest fears and secrets. It might be the awesome present we are excited about giving another friend. Or it could be where we hid something from a sibling. Again, they have information we want to keep private.

For most of us, we trust our parents, spouse, and children more than anyone, and that's a really good thing. Sadly, not everyone can trust those who should be closest to them, but there may be other family members, friends, or other adults you can trust.

Teachers are another group many people trust. This doesn't just mean people in a school. It can mean a martial arts teacher, glass blowing instructor, or sports coach (teacher). It could also be someone like a Scout leader or a youth pastor in church.

Why Trust at All?

Sometimes, bad things happen and you need someone to tell. Sometimes good things happen and you want to share your happiness. It might be something big enough to actually be a crime, or it might be something as small as breaking a glass, but everyone needs help sometimes, even Presidents and Queens. Sometimes your good, exciting news can sound like bragging or no big deal to people who don't know you.

When bad things happen, others may be able to help us fix what went wrong. If you drop a glass and it shatters, and you tell an adult, they should vacuum the area to make sure every last shard is sucked up. That will leave the area safe to walk in. As hard as that might be (since you might get in trouble), it's the right thing to do.

If you drop a glass and it shatters and you pick up the big pieces without telling anyone, there will still be little tiny pieces on the floor. At some point, someone will almost certainly step on them. They could even get a piece stuck in there that gets infected, since only you know the area might have glass shards. (Infection is unlikely, but it is still possible.) Either way, it will hurt. If you had trusted someone enough to ask for help when it broke, that wouldn't have happened.

If you are worried about a big test, you can talk to someone about it—your parents, a teacher or counselor, or a friend. Just talking about it will probably help you feel a little less anxious. If you don't trust anyone enough to talk to them, your anxiety may still go away–but it might get worse because you just keep imagining worse and worse things happening, no matter how unlikely part of you knows it is.

If your painting was selected for the art show, they can go with you to look and share in your excitement. Maybe you'll even win a prize and they'll be there to share in your happiness.

So, we all need to trust other people. We need friends and allies in life to help and support us. If you don't trust anyone else enough to let them get close to you, you will miss out on that help and support. **Life can get very, very lonely if you don't trust anyone.**

Trusting Too Much

With that said, trust makes it easier to hurt us. The amount of damage broken trust can cause depends on how unexpected it was, and how important the item was. That's why it is important to be careful who to trust, especially online.

Conversations that are safe to have with people you know can be dangerous with strangers. The most obvious example is telling someone when your family is traveling. A friend may need to know so they can feed your pets, but posting the information online is an invitation to burglars. You may come home to stolen items, property damage, and the feeling that your home isn't safe anymore.

Similarly, predators can use otherwise harmless information about fights with your parents, school troubles, and other normal bumps in life to worm their way into your confidence. They can drive wedges between you and those who really love you, the very ones you should trust the most, even when you disagree or fight. Your parents, relatives, and close friends will have opinions that differ from yours and think some of your choices are wrong, just like you think some of their choices are wrong. If someone only tells you things you want to hear (or only dwells on the bad things in your life), there is a very good chance they don't have your best interests at heart.

Sometimes, who we can trust changes. I have an aunt who loved me when I was very little. I trusted her. Over the years, something changed. She is now the only person in the family my children never, ever have to stay and visit because she is mean. I have some guesses about what happened, but I don't really know anything beyond it's her, not me. She still loves me, but she damaged my trust beyond repair many years ago. The fact that thinking about my aunt makes my heart hurt now doesn't mean I was wrong to trust her. I can see kindness and loves in old pictures with her. Having long-time friends drop me like last week's trash doesn't mean I was wrong to trust them, either.

How friends behave after the friendship ends tells you whether you were right or wrong to trust them. If you find out they were telling your secrets all along, then you know you were wrong to ever trust them. If, even after the friendship ends, they still keep your secrets, you know you made the right call, no matter how much it hurts now.

While it may not seem like it, almost all friendships end, eventually, and family members drift apart. **A friendship ending, even painfully, doesn't mean you were wrong to trust that person.** It simply means they aren't your go-to person now.

When it *Really* Matters

Sometimes you know something that you simply have to tell someone. It might be that a person is being hurt by someone else or doing something illegal. It might be that you saw something you know is dangerous. Whatever it is, it matters–a lot. You need to tell someone and *soon*.

Hopefully you trust your parents enough to ask them for help. If not, or if you need to act before you see them again, who will you trust?

- Relatives–aunt, uncle, grandparent, cousin
- Teacher–current, past, or other (sometimes you know and trust teachers from camp or siblings' having them)
- Specials' Teacher–art, music, library, counselor, lunch lady, etc.
- Coach
- Scout Leader
- Police Officer/Crossing Guard
- Youth Pastor
- Pastor

- Music Teacher
- Camp Counselor
- Bus Driver
- Neighbor

Personal Information

Know what information simply must be kept secret. Other than banks, the government, employers, schools, and doctors, almost no one needs to know your Social Security Number (SSN). That doesn't mean no one, but it does mean you should be careful who you give it to. Random websites definitely don't need it.

Your SSN is something you should not give to anyone until you are, yourself, an adult. Even as an adult, very few places really need it. Until then, your parents will take care of it for you. This is a very important identifier for US citizens. If someone steals it, it becomes much easier to steal many other things from you, including your money. Guard it well.

Lots of people probably know your birthday, but they are people you know in real life. Again, there is no reason anyone online needs your exact real birthday. A lot of websites will need your age to know how much access to give you and will confirm it with an email. The truth is, as long as your age is pretty close, you don't need to give them your real birthday, just be sure your parents know what you are doing and are OK with it.

My kids have tried to use birthdays that make them as much as three years older. That definitely did not get parental approval! But using their real birthday online would not get my approval either. They generally use dates within six months of their actual age.

It may seem silly, but don't tell people your mom or grandma's maiden name, if you know it. That is her last name before she got married. A lot of places ask for that as a security code. If people get your grandma's maiden name from you, they may be able to use it for identity theft with your parents.

Activity

Most adults have had a trusted friend break that trust at some point. Talk to your parents or another adult you trust about how that feels and whether the friendship was worth it, overall.

Think about adults you trust in your family, at school, in your activities (Scouts, sports, clubs), at your house of worship, and among your friend's parents. You probably won't have someone you truly trust in all those groups, but hopefully you have two or three. Now think about which of your friends you truly, deeply trust.

Is there anything that has been worrying you? Can you talk to one of those people about it? For many problems (including school), an adult's advice is probably best to hear, even if you don't follow it, but if it's a problem at school or with other kids, your friends might have good advice, too.

Quick Quiz

T/F   Never trust anyone.

T/F   People's Social Security Numbers (SSN) are easy to find public records, not private information.

T/F   Someone you trust can turn into someone you shouldn't trust over time.

T/F   Never tell anyone your dad's maiden name.

T/F   Parents and teachers can be good people to trust.

Resources

Articles

Can Your Child Trust You?
http://www.ahaparenting.com/parenting-tools/communication/trust

How to Build Trust
http://www.wikihow.com/Build-Trust

In Teachers We Trust: Can Kids Count on You?
http://www.edutopia.org/blog/trusting-relationships-teachers-students-rebecca-alber

What to Teach Kids about Strangers
http://www.ncpc.org/topics/violent-crime-and-personal-safety/strangers

Scouting-Specific

Youth Protection Training
http://www.scouting.org/Training/YouthProtection.aspx

{Three}

Situational Awareness

No matter what our age, too many of us spend all of our time staring at a screen, even when we're walking around. We have no idea what is happening mere inches from us much less across the street or across town. **We have no awareness of the environment and events going on around us.**

We have no situational awareness.

This is bad.

The simple fact is that most people intend others no harm, but there is no way to look at a person and know which kind they are. **Pay attention to what people say and how they act.** Either one or both can be a red flag warning of danger, but if the two don't match up, that's a warning sign too. That's a good sign they may be lying.

Situational awareness is, at its heart, about observing the details of life around you. Spending time sitting and observing others will help your situational awareness. When you are out in public, sit with your back to a wall, facing everyone else in the room. This will let you observe the room. Make a note of where all the exits are and how you can get there. If anything changes, including people already in the building becoming angry or threatening, or a threatening person enters, you can see it more quickly this way. If you don't sit near the door, you will have even more time to react if someone threatening enters.

Bad Guys preferred prey is oblivious. They want to take the easy route. If you are aware of who and what is around you, then you stop being oblivious.

If a mugger has a choice of two people, one with their head down, focused on their cell (a soft target), and the other with their head up, watching what is happening around them (a hard target), which one do you think they'll chose? That's right, the one where they can grab their purse or wallet and be halfway down the street before their prey looks up, not the one who will see what they are trying to do as they reach their arm out to make the grab. **Be the hard target.**

If you are in a dangerous situation, you will need skills that are covered more thoroughly in Book 2 of this series, *26 Mental & Urban Life Skills*. These include escape and evasion, camouflage, and understanding and recognizing trap points.

The Baseline

Be aware of the baseline (what is normal) for the area you are in. My current home is almost silent except for noises my family makes. My last home had the noise of cars and low-flying jets landing at a nearby airport. Another home had non-stop police and ambulances going by because we lived near an ER.

The level of silence I live with now would have been an indicator of a *major* problem at my other homes. Nothing else would have stopped the traffic flow. But the level that was normal at those homes would only come with some kind of military emergency where I live now. The noise baselines are radically different.

One home has people walk by once or twice an hour, even after dark. Another has them only in the morning and evening. The third has constant traffic flow during daylight hours. The number and closeness of streetlights varied among them, as did the number of neighbors audible through the walls.

Understanding normal levels of pedestrian and vehicle traffic, light, noise, and other environmental variables (including time of day, week, and year) is important to evaluating whether the situation is becoming dangerous. It is a matter of looking at many small things and the way they fit together, like a puzzle.

If you don't know the baseline for an area, it is much harder to recognize when things start going wrong.

Concentric Rings of Disturbance

This is one of the basic theories related to situational awareness. Everyone has seen a rock dropped in water. There is one small ring in the middle and wider (but shallower) ones going out from that starting point in concentric rings. The same thing happens in emergencies. Earthquakes have an epicenter. Tornadoes have paths where they set down. Hurricanes have paths where they hit. Riots have a starting place. Fires have an ignition point. Accidents have an impact point.

Whatever the emergency, *there is a starting point* and other, lesser, waves of damage radiate out from that point. **The farther you can be from that starting point when the emergency starts, the safer you will be.** Period. If you live near the center, the faster and farther you get away, the better.

Environmental Clues

Imagine it is raining and you travel over a bridge. One of two things happens.

- The driver is absorbed with singing along to the radio and doesn't notice the water starting to wash over the road.
- When you return an hour later, the area is flooded. You can't get home until the water recedes, days or even weeks later. Your cats are very angry.

OR

- After noticing standing water on the road, the driver turns off the music to focus on not hydroplaning. (This is when the car wheels slide on top of water on the road instead of sticking to the road surface.)
- Carefully watching the road surface and driving conditions, the driver immediately notices the water washing across parts of the bridge. As they slow down and scan to the side, they see the stream of water under the bridge has swollen to within inches of the surface. You turn around and go home without ever crossing the bridge.

There are lots of little clues like this before things occur as well as after. Sherlock Holmes was the (fictional) master of this. **Learning to read small clues like the standing water in the road and the water washing over the bridge can do a lot to keep you safe.**

Animals are very good at this. It helps keep them alive in the wild. Observing animals is a good way to improve your situational awareness. If a lot of animals are running in a specific direction, it's a good bet you should follow them.

Smells can be great environmental cues. The smell of barbeque alerts us to a nearby cookout. The smell of wood smoke can be soothing if we are camping, but a danger sign if there is a wildfire in the area. Burning rubber and most truly nasty smells (not including skunk, since that hangs around seemingly forever) are a solid warning that something potentially dangerous is nearby. Avoid them.

Focus Lock

Fight the tendency to let one big thing grab all your focus and lock it in, leaving you unaware of everything else going on around you. That includes your electronic gadgets and talking with friends. This is especially true in transition areas, areas which are neither one thing nor the other. Hallways are a transition between rooms. Garages, sidewalks, and paths are transitions between your transportation and your destination.

The hallway in your home is unlikely to be a dangerous area, but the hallways in schools, hotels, and other public areas are spaces where someone could rob or attack you. Garages are notorious as places people are attacked because they are generally isolated and people tend to be distracted, thus easy prey.

Bad Guys use distractions to force a focus lock. If you are walking down the street and someone starts arguing loudly in front of you, it's hard to not focus on it, but if you do, someone else can come up behind you or from the side and attack you or steal from you. Likewise, someone can block your path and force you to go somewhere less safe. If you keep your focus locked straight ahead, they have an easy time attacking from their preferred location: the side.

If you are looking around and aware of your surroundings, most Bad Guys will wait for the next person who isn't. It probably won't be a long wait.

Human Clues

Pay attention to what people are and are not doing, and how they are different from the baseline for the area. This is critical for good situational awareness.

Activity

As you drive through a normally busy neighborhood, there are no people on the street, but a few seem to be peeking out their windows.

- They may have heard others talking and know violence is about to happen.
- They may have just seen something violent happen.
- They may have heard a weather report or storm warning that dangerous weather is on the way.

The normal groups of kids are gathered in front of the building after school, but instead of texting and chatting they are yelling at each other and look angry.

- A fight may be about to break out.
- Something bad may have happened elsewhere that they are upset about.

The home improvement store has a steady stream of people coming out the door with large sheets of plywood. There aren't many reasons for this other than people are boarding up their homes.

- The most likely reason is that a big storm in on the way.

- Another possibility is that something on the news that makes them fear rioting may happen, and soon.

Emotions

There will always be people who are happy, sad, angry, silly–the whole gamut of human emotion–at any given time. When everyone is reacting the same way, especially a negative emotion, that should be a red flag that makes you stop and take notice.

If you notice a group of people who seem agitated, angry, or fearful, quickly and quietly move away to a safe place. Do not try to help them. There are people who have been trained to do that, like the police.

Scenarios and Possible Explanations

There don't seem to be any police around.

- When big storms hit, accidents increase, requiring extra police to respond. Many police forces let extra staff have time off just before a big storm hits so they have a rested, alert force available.
- When controversial legal decisions are announced, there can be riots and other disturbances and, again, more police are needed, so they let officers have off beforehand.
- When there are big events like the Boston Marathon, Academy Awards, and DC Cherry Blossom Festival, more police are needed so they schedule accordingly.

- They may all be responding to some very large event in another area.

All the people in all the stores are buying random helmets and baseball bats/fire pokers/golf clubs.

- The Zombie Apocalypse has started. They want to protect their brains while being able to beat back zombies.

Kids on the bus are talking about causing trouble.

- Are they sitting at the back of the bus where it's harder for the driver to watch them? Troublemakers tend to.
- Is there a bus monitor on board? Are they nearby?
- See if the other kids seem to notice or care, if they look uncomfortable, or if they are moving away from the troublemakers.
- Notice who is involved in the conversation, but be sure not to stare at them or draw attention to yourself. Don't write down their names, just try to remember them. You don't want to accidentally put yourself in danger.
- Talk to your parents about it and don't sit near those kids on the bus for a while. You may want to find another form of transportation for a bit, even just riding a different bus with a friend.

When large groups of people behave oddly, there is usually a reason. Good situational awareness helps you notice the behavior and figure out the cause. It may be nothing to be concerned about, such as when stores have few customers on Sunday morning (they're at church), or it might indicate a very dangerous situation (an oncoming hurricane).

Practice

When you see an accident on the road, see what you can observe as you go past. (This isn't advising slowing down to be a lookie-loo, just what you see as a passenger passing by at a normal speed.)

- Where is the vehicle crumpled?
- Are emergency vehicles (police, fire, ambulance) and crew there? What are they doing?
- Is there debris on the road? Where?
- Are other vehicles involved?

The crumpled part of the car provides clues about where and how it was hit. If a car is hit straight-on from the back, the rear-end will be fairly uniformly smashed into the trunk. If the person who hit it swerved or was turning, damage will be off to one side.

Debris on the road tells you approximately where the vehicle(s) was at the time of collision. A tow-truck tells you the car isn't drivable. Emergency crews standing calmly and not doing much tell you either no one was seriously injured, or they have already gone to the hospi-tal–probably the former–because they don't have work to do.

SITUATIONAL AWARENESS

Activity

Go somewhere with a lot of people, like a park or a mall, with your parents or another adult. Spend some time just watching them and trying to guess what they will do and something about them as people. Talk about what each of you thinks and why.

Close your eyes. Have the person with you ask questions about the people and your general surroundings, or simply describe what you saw. How observant were you? Try switching places. If you ask questions first, do you do a better job of remembering details?

How many of your thoughts about other people, and even your observations of the area, are based on your personal experiences and how many are based on the way the TV, internet, YouTube, or games portray people and communities?

Quick Quiz

T/F   Only big details are part of situational awareness.

T/F   Situational awareness can help you stay safe from danger.

T/F   Situational awareness only matters when you know you are in danger.

T/F   Situational awareness is only about what you see.

T/F   Sherlock Holmes had no situational awareness.

Resources

Articles

*3 Effective Techniques to Train Your Situational Awareness and Recognize Change
http://www.itstactical.com/intellicom/mindset/3-effective-techniques-to-train-your-situational-awareness-and-recognize-change/

*How to Develop the Situational Awareness of Jason Bourne
http://www.artofmanliness.com/2015/02/05/how-to-develop-the-situational-awareness-of-jason-bourne/

Situational Awareness
http://www.thedailysheeple.com/situational-awareness_102014

Situational Awareness: A Key to Your Safety
http://www.huffingtonpost.com/avital-zeisler/situational-awareness-a-k_b_4846700.html

Situational Awareness Matters
http://www.samatters.com/

Books

Escaping the O Zone: Intuition, Situational Awareness and Staying Safe by Doug M. Cummings

Scouting-Specific

Special Agent Badge
http://forgirls.girlscouts.org/home/badgeexplorer/#special-agent

Videos

*Brian's Game: A Lesson in Situational Awareness
https://www.youtube.com/watch?v=xcI2ar-fVOE

Situational Awareness and Tunnel Vision
https://www.youtube.com/watch?v=EG6NyCDN-Ts

{Four}

Problem Solving

This is a very basic skill. In school, problem solving is usually straight forward because there is a teacher with you, defining the problem that needs solved. **In real life, determining what the problem *is* is often the first step in problem solving.**

Why it Matters

The most obvious reason is that problem solving enables you to solve problems. This isn't about solving *a* problem, singular. It's about developing the skills to work on solving *all kinds* of problems, and the basic steps are the same whether its' about sharing a toy in preschool or admitting it's time to move to assisted living as a senior citizen.

The less obvious reason is that good problem solving skills help reduce stress and fighting. How's that? **A truly good problem solver takes time to understand the source of the problem and resolve that, not just the symptoms,** so that even if everyone isn't happy, at least they aren't mad and don't feel unfairly treated.

Everyone knows stepping on Lego™ *hurts*. I kept making my eldest pick up the Lego pieces spread all over the floor, right where we walk. Ten minutes later, the floor was covered with Lego (again). I was only treating the symptom. Eventually, I sat down and talked to him.

He wanted the Lego spread out to see all the pieces and be inspired to create amazing things. That just wasn't going to work for the rest of the family, but now I knew the reason he kept spreading the Lego everywhere. Instead of continuing to get mad, I moved the Lego into a new storage solution with open bins so he could see all the different kinds of pieces.

Now, the pieces are (mostly) confined to bins, it's a lot faster to clean up, and there are a lot less hurt feet. Problem solving led us to a solution everyone can live with, even though it isn't anyone's ideal.

Steps

1. Identify problem.

2. Find possible causes/sources (brainstorm).

3. List potential paths of action (brainstorm).

4. Evaluate choices.

5. Choose one and try it.

6. Evaluate solution used.

7. If it was not fixed, go back to Step 2 to make sure nothing important was missed and repeat the process until it is fixed or no longer matters.

Moving the Lego to the bins helped immensely, but we still had some Lego in the walking path. This led me to taking the next step of moving the Lego farther from the walking path. The area then started collecting cat fur and was very difficult to keep tolerably clean (the Lego or the floor), so we moved it to yet another spot. Finally, it has a happy home that works for everyone.

We had to go through the whole process several times, but each one moved us to a better spot and closer to a final resolution.

A Real-Life Example

The water in our house has been cutting out. The first step was determining if it was a one-time thing or an ongoing problem. It could have been some kind of clog in the pipes that worked its way loose. Alas, it was not. It was an ongoing problem in need of solving.

The next step was to look for more details to zero in on the source of the problem. Was there a leak in a pipe? Was a piece of plumbing equipment damaged or otherwise not working? Was anything visible (or audible) in the house to help determine the location of the problem? Some possible causes would have required calling a plumber (repairing a major pipe or repairing the water heater), some were easy DIY (Do It Yourself) fixes (minor leaks, changing clogged filters), and others required the well guys. (For city water, substitute "main line guys" for "well guys" throughout this example.)

After changing the dirty water filters and confirming there were no leaks anywhere in the house, the next step was observing when it happened, and where. If the problem was only on one floor of the house or in one room, we would have known it was a plumbing problem. Since it affected the whole house equally, we knew the well was almost certainly the problem.

After gathering all the possible data, consider the possibilities. In this case, it's either a plumbing problem inside the house or a problem with the well and/or well line to the house. Since the entire house was affected equally and all the pipes inside were fine, the natural conclusion was that it was a well problem and we needed to call the well guys.

We also determined that it is much worse when we use the outside hose (*lots* of water at once), so we looked into whether it could be a part on the well pump. It turned that a lightning strike damaged our well pump and it needed replaced.

If we hadn't taken the time to look at all the possible causes, we could have wasted time and money calling the plumber out to look at something that is definitely not a plumbing issue.

Activity

Play the "What If" game. What if your microwave catches on fire? What if your Grandma buys you an ugly sweater? What if a time-traveling alien takes your entire school and puts it on the moon? Come up with your own "What If" questions and solve those problems!

OR

Find a problem in your life or community and go through this process. It may be which classes or clubs you choose to join, or a bigger issue such as promoting world peace. Practicing on something theoretical is entirely OK.

Quick Quiz

T/F   Good problem solving skills can help reduce stress.

T/F   The first step in problem solving is coming up with a solution.

T/F   Problem solving is only useful in school.

T/F   Brainstorming is always part of problem solving.

T/F   We don't need to do problem solving very often.

Resources

Articles

Developing Critical Thinking Skills in Children
http://www.brighthorizons.com/family-resources/e-family-news/2014-developing-critical-thinking-skills-in-children/

How to Help Children Develop Problem Solving Skills
http://missourifamilies.org/features/parentingarticles/parenting81.htm

Books

Problem Solving: Proven Strategies to Mastering Critical Thinking, Problem Solving and Decision Making by Thomas Richards

Scouting-Specific

Truth Seeker Badge
http://forgirls.girlscouts.org/home/badgeexplorer/#truth-seeker

Videos

Activities to Teach Problem Solving to Children
https://www.youtube.com/watch?v=RsaHoy-WeoI

Always a Solution (Problem Solving for Kids) Vol 2
https://www.youtube.com/watch?v=NeOGRJvP50g

{Five}

Plan Ahead

Think ahead and always have a plan. Even a very basic plan like "duck and cover" or "run and hide" is better than nothing. What disasters or emergencies could happen to you? How can you be prepared for each one?

At School

If you are homeschooled, skip to the next section.

Schools are required to do a certain number of drills every year, including fire and lock-down drills, at a minimum. Others, such as tornado and earthquake drills, are based on local conditions. What kinds does your school have? Are you comfortable with the drills? If not, talk to your parents and teachers to find a way to make it easier.

One boy I know has very sensitive hearing and the alarms *hurt*. It made it harder to listen to the teacher and follow instructions. Some teachers would let him cover his ears, other said it wasn't OK. After confirming with the principal that it was OK, he was able to tell any teacher who objected that the principal said it was OK and he didn't have any further problems.

If the alarms go off and it isn't a drill, can you handle that? If there really was a fire in your school, what would you do?

If school is evacuated, do you wear clothing that would keep you safe outside, possibly for hours? A lot of kids like to go to school wearing shorts, flip flops, and/or light-weight jackets even when it's 20°F outside. If you wore that and the school was evacuated, how would your body feel? If it was 15 minutes versus 2 hours, what difference would that make?

No school would have a drill when it is that cold outside, but the cold weather can cause real problems like a roof collapse from heavy snow, burst pipes, or furnace problems, and real emergencies can happen at any time of the year. Knowing what you would do in advance will help you if it ever really happens.

At Home

We are all told to do fire drills in our house and know where to meet outside as a family if there is an emergency and we have to flee. Do you do drills? Do you know how to escape your bedroom? Do you know where to meet? What if your entire neighborhood or even town is gone–perhaps burnt down or flattened? Have a family meeting to review your plans and update any weaknesses, then carry out a practice family fire drill.

Do you know what to do if there is a tornado, earthquake, flood, or other natural disaster in your area? Where will you meet your family or emergency responders if you have to flee from your home? What will you take with you?

Some homes are designed and built specifically to withstand specific disasters (hurricane, tornado, earthquake, home invasion), and others have "safe rooms" to shelter the people in a disaster. Since most homes don't have anything like that, when the phrase "safe room" is used in this section, it refers to the safest room in your house, assuming that you don't have a purpose-built "safe room."

If you live in an area where any kind of disasters or emergencies are common, you should have a list prepared of what to pack for an evacuation. Keep it in a drawer where you can find it quickly and easily. Don't forget to update it, especially when you change schools! Some items can be pre-packed so you can just grab them and go. Important papers (discussed later in this chapter) are an example of this.

Earthquake

Do you know where your family earthquake kit is? Do you know how to turn off the gas and where the gadget to do so is? That could keep your home safe.

What is the safest place in your home? Are there strong doorways? A tub to hide in? Strong furniture to crouch under? How long should you stay there? Where should you go next? How do you know if it's safe to stay in the building?

Should you run outside? If so, should you wait until things stop moving? If you go outside, what dangers are nearby? Some homes have electrical wires or other buildings near them. Some have lots of open space. Have some idea of what might fall down or roll toward you (including cars parked on a hill) and be a danger in an earthquake.

Fire

Schools cover this a lot and so do many other organizations. Stop, drop, and roll remains excellent advice. If your clothing happens to start to catch fire, then rolling helps to put it out. Running around flapping your arms makes it worse. Fire needs oxygen for fuel and this extra movement provides the fire with more air. Rolling around deprives it of oxygen.

Dropping down low also puts you below the worst of the smoke from the fire and that is one of the most important pieces of advice in a fire: **stay low to avoid the smoke**. Smoke inhalation is the most common way to die in a fire, far more common than burning to death.

If you are in a room and it starts to fill with smoke, block the bottom of the door with anything you can to keep the smoke out. Cover your mouth and nose with something like a neckerchief or facemask, even a t-shirt. It will filter out at least some of the smoke and ash particles. Wetting it with water from a sink, bottle, or whatever (even a can of soda) helps it remove even more ash.

If either the door or doorknob is hot, then the fire is very close and opening the door is very dangerous. Find another way out.

Once you are outside, go to the designated meeting place. That might be your mailbox, the end of the driveway, or a neighbor's house, but make sure it is far enough from your house that sparks from the fire can't land on you. When emergency services arrive, let them know you are out and safe and tell them if anyone else is still inside the house, including pets. **Do not go looking for pets yourself.** Scared animals hide and you don't want to be hurt yourself while you are looking for a pet that may be in a tiny spot no human can reach.

Flood

Where should you go if a flood threatens your home and you are trapped there? Is there a high spot on your property that is safe? Does is have a building for you to shelter in? If so, make sure to take some supplies (food, water, blankets, flashlights/lanterns, etc.) so you are comfortable.

If there is no higher spot and flood waters are coming into your home, can you get onto the roof, maybe a porch roof? How will you do that? Ask an adult for help learning how to do that and showing you where any tools you need are kept.

Do you have a canoe or boat you can use to escape? If so, what will go in it with you? If you plan on taking pets with you, remember that most will need a cage to keep them from panicking and jumping out.

Hurricane

Hurricanes give more advance notice than most potential disasters. You and your family have the chance to board up the windows and doors to keep them from exploding and to gather important items and evacuate before it hits, although evacuation can turn into a disaster in its own right if the storm is big enough.

Make sure to pay attention to hurricane watches and warnings. Talk to your parents about any that are coming near you. If there is a mandatory evacuation, evacuate. Just go.

If something happens and you are stuck somewhere that is being hit by a hurricane, go to the most hurricane-safe room in the building. (See the instructions for a tornado-safe room in the next section to determine which room that is.) Stay there.

At some point, all the storm noise (wind, rain, blowing debris) will stop and it will sound safe to leave the safe room. That is called the eye of the storm. While no one really disputes that it is safe during the eye, the problem is that this is a temporary lull and the full force of the storm will hit again with little or no warning. Do yourself and those who love you a favor: don't venture out of the safe room during the eye of the storm for any reason.

Tornado

Where is the tornado-safe room or place in your house? Here are some characteristics to keep in mind for a tornado-safe room:

- windowless
- interior
- on a lower floor
- nothing large or heavy directly overhead

- strong walls a plus

The CDC recommends the inside (center) of a basement or, if you don't have a usable basement, the lowest floor of the building.

Have you seen the commercial about how many licks does it take to get to the center of a lollipop? It takes so long they bite into it to get there faster. It's sort of like that with a house getting destroyed. The roof tends to go first, ripped out from underneath by the wind. Rooms on the top floor start being pulled apart. Windows get blown out, especially if they aren't covered. Rooms on the outside start flying apart. **Like the center of the lollipop, the center of the house, and the floors closer to the ground, last longest.**

Once the tornado hits, hide under a heavy piece of furniture such as a table or desk. Protecting your head and body from flying debris is important and the table or desk will help do that. Covering your head with your hands is also a good idea. If you are in a room with a mattress or large cushions, those can also help protect your body from flying debris if you cover yourself with them.

This is when not having anything large or heavy directly overhead can be important. An a/c unit or piano falling on a person is Very Bad.

Emergency Bag /Bug Out Bag

This is called by many different names, but it is the bag you will take if you have to evacuate (leave home) quickly. Adults can leave clothing and shoes packed in theirs all the time, but anyone who is still growing is better off having a list of things to pack to make sure they are the right size.

Each person, no matter their age, needs to be responsible for packing their own items for evacuation. Packing your own bag makes it easier to find things and to remember what is there. It also gives you a chance to tailor it to suit yourself. Mom gave you peanut butter bars but you wanted chocolate chip? Swap 'em out. The socks have a seam that hurts? Toss 'em and get a better pair. Go ahead and add a tablet and pencil if you like to sketch to pass the time. This gives you the chance to do some small things you need to personalize it.

Clothing and Toiletries

The basics include socks, underwear, shirts, and pants/skirts. Include enough for as long as your parents tell you, but one week is probably good. You also need seasonal clothing including a swimsuit, rain jacket, winter jacket/gloves/snowsuit, and a hat (baseball or ski, depending on the season). Shoes should be sturdy, not cute or fun. Sneakers are a must. If you have hiking boots (rain or snow boots too, in season), that's even better. But make sure they are broken in.

Toiletries can be pre-packed. You definitely need a toothbrush, toothpaste, and dental floss. The samples from a visit to the dentist are perfect for this. Complimentary hotel toiletries of soap, shampoo, and conditioner (if you use it) are also idea. The travel-size section of most pharmacy departments includes deodorant, disposable razors, hair bands. and many other things you, personally, might need.

Important Papers

Adults have a very long list of important papers to take with them. Kids have a much shorter list, but that doesn't mean it isn't important. Here are some basic papers you should have copies of that you can grab to take with you in an emergency.

- **Address list:** If you get lost, this can help you get to where you are going or to friends along the way who can help you.

- **Birth certificate, social security card, and passport** (if you have one): This proves your citizenship and residency. In addition to the traditional passport book, it is now possible to get a passport card that is the same size and shape as a state ID/driver's license. It can only be used for land border crossings, which limits its usefulness.

- **School id:** This shows more specifically where you are from and, unlike birth certificates and social security cards, these are generally photo ids.

- **Medical records:** If you end up in an emergency shelter and don't have proof of vaccinations, you may be forced to retake some or all of them. If you have medical problems or need medication, doctor's records will make it far easier to get help while you are displaced.

- **Parents' id and recent photo:** If you become separated from your parents, this should help you become reunited more quickly. (Remember: These are primarily copies, not the originals.)

CHAPTER FIVE

Packing List

This is primarily for situations where you are evacuating, like a hurricane, wild fire, or flood threatening your home. Start off with the items listed above. Then add the items you use every day and would definitely need to take with you in an emergency.

- **Electronics and Chargers:** Cell phone, tablet, laptop, put any electronics you use all the time and can't do without on the list with all the cords and chargers you need. If you have a solar charger, bring that as well. If not, consider adding one to your wish list.
- **Medicine:** In an emergency, even something as simple as aspirin for a headache or motion sickness medicine could be hard to find, so pack anything you use often. Definitely pack any prescription medicine, such as an asthma inhaler, that you need.
- **Food:** You won't want to bring massive amounts, but you probably will want to have your first meal and some snacks. If your parents pack the, there is no guarantee you will like it. If you pack it, your parents may fuss that it isn't healthy, but at least you will like it. Be sure to pack cold packs if you have anything that really needs to stay cold, like a turkey sandwich.
- **Water:** Your parents should pack a minimum of a case of water if you are evacuating, but that may be in the back. Go ahead and pack your own favorite non-leaky water bottle and keep it with you. That also helps guarantee you know which one is yours.

Visiting

Is there someone you visit regularly, like your grandparents, a close friend, or a favorite aunt? What would you do for each of those scenarios if were visiting their house? Are there any things you need to do differently at their home(s)? Are there different disasters you need to be prepared for than at your own home?

Weather

Check the weather forecast regularly. Some people watch the weather on TV, others use an app, and still others use a website. Whatever your preferred method, you should be aware of the expected weather for the next 3-5 days, tomorrow, today, and possibly hourly, depending on what is in the forecast, the season, and what you will be doing.

If you are in an area where hurricanes, snowstorms, or other large storms that can be predicted days or even a week or more (in a few instances) are "in season," then you should definitely pay attention to at least the 3-5 day forecast, if not the admittedly far less reliable ten day forecast. If something big enough to potentially leave you stuck at home is in the forecast, then you have enough time to be prepared.

Even if there isn't anything big in offing, watching the forecast helps us all to plan our activities. It's no fun hauling bags of groceries into the house in a downpour or in 100+ heat, but it's even less fun to be outside doing chores or going on a bike-hike in those conditions. It especially sucks if the weather the day before or earlier in the same day was perfect.

Timing when to do things within a day is the best reason to check the hourly forecasts. If you want to do something outside like bike riding but there is rain in the forecast for the day, look at the hourly forecast. It might not be expected until early or even late afternoon, leaving plenty of time to go earlier in the day–IF you know and get out in time.

Activity

Discuss with an adult what you should do in the following situations:

- You smell gas.
- You see sparks.
- You see fire.
- A closed door or doorknob feels hot, and not just like the sun has been shining on it.
- You smell or see smoke. How should you respond differently if it's from dinner burning or an unknown cause?
- You see water dripping from somewhere it shouldn't, like the ceiling or a pipe, or a stain spreading on the ceiling. (The stain is probably from dripping water.)
- You are stuck outside in the cold or heat. How does having or not having a phone affect this?
- There is a natural disaster known to affect your area, whether that is an earthquake, a tsunami, a snow storm, or a flood.
- You are outside and see a dangerous animal, including certain snakes and spiders.

PLAN AHEAD

Make a list of any skills you need to work, items you need to buy/find/make, information you need (e.g., where the gas shut off and shut off tool are), and people you might need to talk to (e.g., a neighbor whose house you should run to in an emergency).

Quick Quiz

T/F   It's a good idea to think about how you would react in an emergency when you are at the home of someone you visit someone often, like a grandparent or best friend.

T/F   Watching the weather forecast helps us plan ahead.

T/F   The way we react to an emergency depends, in part, on where we are.

T/F   Once you have done two or three emergency drills, it isn't important to participate any more.

T/F   The weather forecast only really matters in the winter, when it might become really cold outside.

Resources

Articles
Planning Skills
http://learningworksforkids.com/skills/planning/

Residential Safe Rooms
https://www.fema.gov/safe-rooms/residential-safe-rooms

Books

Smart but Scattered: The Revolutionary "Executive Skills" Approach to Helping Kids Reach Their Potential by Peg Dawson

Smart but Scattered Teens: The "Executive Skills" Program for Helping Teens Reach Their Potential by Richard Guare Ph.D.

Scouting-Specific

Home Repair Merit Badge
http://meritbadge.org/wiki/index.php/Home_Repairs

Safety Merit Badge
http://meritbadge.org/wiki/index.php/Safety

Weather Merit Badge
http://meritbadge.org/wiki/index.php/Weather

Videos

Executive Functions for Kids
https://www.youtube.com/watch?v=REo3fzja5xs

InBrief: Executive Function: Skills for Life and Learning
https://www.youtube.com/watch?v=efCq_vHUMqs

{Six}

Dress for the Weather

If you are like a lot of teens, you may think you can safely wear shorts and flip flops outside even in the middle of a Siberian winter. That is survivable if the only "outside" time is between the front door and (warm) car and from the car into a warm building. It won't work in an emergency.

Learning to dress appropriately for the weather conditions could save your life, literally. My kids catch the bus at the end of our driveway and walk a *very* short distance into their school building. This leads them to believe that even if it is -4°F with wind-chill outside, they only need a light jacket. After all, they won't be exposed long.

While that's not wrong, what happens if the bus breaks down or the school needs evacuated outside? A local school had part of their roof collapse from the weight of snow. If it had happened during school instead of at night, those kids would have been outside in the freezing weather for at least an hour. Some might have been injured or even killed not just by the falling roof but also by exposure to the extreme cold. Wearing just that thin jacket in truly cold weather could be quite dangerous.

As a teen, you might not want to wear a bulky jacket when it seems so unlikely that something bad will happen, especially if your locker is small. And you are right that it probably won't, but your house probably won't catch fire and you still have smoke detectors. Wearing a warm jacket or keeping one in your locker won't hurt you but *not* wearing it could, if it is truly a safety matter like wearing a jacket designed for mid 40°s when it's -4°.

To convince my son, I threatened to show up at his bus after school with his coat, loudly explaining that I was his mommy, so I was bringing my forgetful little love bug the jacket he forgot at home.

As a middle-schooler, my son viewed the potential humiliation in much the same way I viewed him standing outside for an hour in that jacket. And he knows me well enough to know that it wasn't a bluff, so he wears the warm jacket when I tell him he must. Mission accomplished.

Layering

Layering is the most important part of dressing for the weather. No matter what the season or where you are, the temperature changes throughout the day and you must be prepared for all eventualities.

If you look closely at the windows in your house, they are probably either single or double pane. Almost all old windows are single pane and almost all new ones are double pane, thanks to advances in technology. Most double pane windows have a layer of gas in the middle that acts as insulation so the cold outside air doesn't lower the temperature inside your home as quickly. If you have some of each, you can feel the difference in how much cold (or heat) gets through.

Layers of clothing act the same way. Each layer allows some air space between it and the next one, unless it's really tight. Your body heats up the layers of fabric and the air pockets in between, helping keep the cold away from your skin.

Do you ever wear a sweatshirt with a t-shirt under it in cold weather? A t-shirt by itself doesn't do much to keep you warm and a sweatshirt alone isn't terribly warm either, but if you pair them, it somehow makes a *huge* difference in how warm you remain. This is because of the two pockets of warmed up air, a smaller one between the t-shirt and your body and a larger one between your t-shirt and sweatshirt.

Layering is good in hot weather as well as cold. You won't want to wear a lot of layers when it is hot out, but it always gets cooler in the evening, in the shade, and when you go into an air conditioned building. In addition, a loose outer layer can help keep you cooler.

Cold Weather

If you wear a loose bottom layer, there will be that pocket of air between your body and that fabric that your body can warm up in the same way that a furnace warms a room. For this reason, it's better if the base layer isn't skin-tight. You do want a small amount of space.

There are some great new performance fabrics. Wool is now and has always been one of the best choices for survivability. Some kinds of wool are very hot and very itchy, but "some" is most definitely not all. Some types of wool, such as merino wool, are far less itchy, and wool socks are rarely itchy. In addition, wool can be spun to be quite thin and lightweight.

Different types of wool come from different breeds of sheep, just like there are different breeds of dogs and cats. As with any other animal, some have softer fur and others are more bristly. The softer kinds are generally more expensive.

Damp

Damp clothing can lead to a multitude of problems, if not fixed reasonably quickly, especially when it's not hot. Some causes are obvious, such as rain or falling in a pond, others are not as obvious. Sweating, as discussed below, is one. Another is condensation inside a tent, if you don't leave an opening for ventilation when you are inside it.

Hot Weather

Some fabrics breath, some don't. Those that don't make you sweat–a lot. The best fabrics are natural fibers such as linen and cotton, and some newer man-made wicking "performance" fabrics. These new fabrics can be great. So can wool, as contrary as that seems. There are very light-weight wools now and wool still protects you even when it's wet. Wet cotton just feels clammy, and nylon is even worse.

A very loose top layer can be a good way to stay cool. Have you ever seen a picture of a Bedouin? They live in the Sahara desert and would know better than almost anyone what to wear to stay cool in the heat. They wear long flowing robes and head-coverings as their top layer. Only their faces, or even just their eyes, are visible to protect them from the extreme heat, burning sand, and sun.

Finally, colors matter in the heat. Black absorbs heat. White reflects heat. The darker your clothing, the hotter you are likely to get. The lighter it is, the cooler it is.

Sweating and High Humidity

It may seem counter-intuitive, but even when it's cold outside, the human body perspires. That's an important concept for survival, because people who don't allow for it may let their clothing and their sleeping gear to became damp, which is unhealthy and could be dangerous, particularly in the cold.

This is another reason layering is so important. When you are active and start sweating and over-heating, it is easy to take off layers. As you finish and start to cool down, simply put them back on.

Wind and Rain

It might seem like the best choice is a rubber coat and pants rain set, but they don't breathe. That means you'll sweat, which means you'll get damp. And we've already covered what that will do. But they definitely keep the rain out.

Even so, if it's truly wet, sometimes it's better to get a little sweaty and damp inside the rubber than to get well and truly drenched by Mother Nature. Sweatiness isn't really a factor if you will only be wearing it for a short time. That's why sailors in massive gales are often pictured in full rubber suits: a wave washing over you will assuredly get you more thoroughly drenched than sweating.

When I was caught in a downpour in college, I wore a black garbage bag as a rain poncho to go back to my dorm without being soaked. It looked silly, but it worked! Today, you can pick up a lightweight, cheap rain poncho almost anywhere and keep it in your bag. They work and there is enough space under them to keep you from getting all sweaty and nasty from wearing it.

The true advantage to plastic and rubber rain gear is, quite simply, their price. They are dirt cheap compared to breathable water-proof fabrics. The other problem with the breathable water-proof fabrics is that the newest fabrics really aren't widely available in youth sizes, probably because of their price.

Activity

Now that you know how to safely dress for all different kinds of weather, go to www.weather.gov and look at the weather forecast for where you will be during the next week. Decide what clothing you should wear, that you already own, to stay safe in that weather, even if a broken down vehicle forced you to walk a mile or two for help.

Now think about what kind of weather you can expect in six months. How would you dress differently for that weather? Is there anything you don't own or can't find for either situation?

If you grow six inches in the next six months, will you still have everything you need? If so, great job to you and your parents! If not, make a list and keep an eye out for bargains on those items.

P.S. Do your parents and siblings have everything they need?

Quick Quiz

T/F   In cold weather, you want your base layer tight against your skin.

T/F   Sweating can be an issue even when it is very cold.

T/F   Never wear layers in cold weather.

T/F   Staying damp for too long can lead to a variety of sicknesses and health problems.

T/F   A full rubber rain suit is always the best choice in the rain.

Resources

Articles

Fabrics to Keep You Cool
http://www.goodhousekeeping.com/institute/a3004/fabrics-to-keep-you-cool/

How to Dress for the Cold
http://www.wikihow.com/Dress-for-the-Cold

How to Stay Cool in Warm Weather
http://www.wikihow.com/Stay-Cool-in-Warm-Weather

CHAPTER SIX

*Introduction to Layered Clothing Systems
http://www.outdoorgearlab.com/a/11061/Introduction-to-Layered-Clothing-Systems

REI: Layering Basics
http://www.rei.com/learn/expert-advice/layering-basics.html

What are the Best Fabrics to Wear in Tropical Climates?
http://www.wisegeek.org/what-are-the-best-fabrics-to-wear-in-tropical-climates.htm

Videos

Cold Weather Dressing Tips–Base Layer Insulating Layers–Extreme Arctic Clothing
https://www.youtube.com/watch?v=uVQ0KcHjZrY

How to Dress for Cold-Weather Running
https://www.youtube.com/watch?v=8eC5toC0vms

*How to Dress for Cold Weather Cycling by Performance Bicycle
https://www.youtube.com/watch?v=1F6AmmT2X7c

*Winter Warmth–Winter Layering System
https://www.youtube.com/watch?v=Y-5xJh8jSg4

{Seven}

Physical Fitness

We've all heard it before: we need to exercise more. You can bike, run, hike, swim, or any of the other hundreds or thousands of activities out there, but some exercise is more helpful for disaster preparedness than others.

It's fairly simple, like many other things: If you aren't physically fit, you won't fare well in an emergency.

As much as I love my dancing video games, they are definitely not something that will help in emergency preparedness. Yoga won't do much either, although it helps with remaining mentally alert and calm. If you have trouble motivating yourself to exercise, try joining a group or club to make it a social activity.

Many of the tasks we have automated today can be done as easily, or nearly as easily, by hand. Do you use an electric can opener? A hand-held one is smaller, fits easily in a drawer, and is dishwasher safe. You can use a whisk or pastry blender for most of what an electric mixer does. Admittedly not all that it does, but a lot of it.

Swapping electric items out for hand powered ones means not only that you can are physically active and engaged in the task, but if the power goes out, you don't have to change that part of how you cook. You have also developed muscle memory for using those tools. A family friend had many years of competitive gymnastics training (rings), up through college. When he was thrown from a motorcycle in an accident decades later, his muscle memory helped him land safely because he automatically tucked and rolled. Using a whisk isn't a life-or-death situation, but with practice, you will become more efficient with these tools.

These changes won't make a noticeable difference in energy usage, but it does make a mental difference. If you are used to having everything you do from opening a can to heating your home to watering the grass automated, then you spend more of your time sitting physically idle. (To be clear, I am firmly in favor of central heating and air conditioning; home heating is just an example of something that required a lot of physical labor as recently as 100 years ago.) You also lack the muscle memory to those tasks as quickly and efficiently when it really matters.

Dressing for the weather (Chapter 6) is extremely important for physical exercise. That chapter includes several links and videos related to appropriate dressing for physical activity.

Biking

Bike riding is a great way to keep in shape and get around. It is great fun for teens and parents alike. Learning how to check your bike and make basic repairs is important. Decent shoes, a properly fitted helmet, and clothing that won't get caught in the bike chains are all important even on short rides. Having a bottle of water is important for pretty much anything more than a ride around the block.

There are great bike trails all over the world! Do you need somewhere new to bike ride or hike? Check out your local visitor's bureau. They often have lists of local trails for bike riding and hiking. (The trails can be one and the same.) Many areas have historic and nature trails to explore and geo-caching can add a lot of fun and challenges. An internet search should help you find even more.

Chores

Many chores and other physical activities both exercise your body and accomplish a task you need done such as splitting wood (yes, people still do that) or shoveling snow.

Yardwork isn't easily automated (other than sprinklers), and even small yards generate surprisingly large amounts of work. Mowing, possibly with a hand mower (just not for a ten acre plot!), is a good way to get outside and get started with yardwork, once you are big and strong enough to handle the mower. Pulling weeds is something even the smallest toddler can handle, with supervision. Virtually every yard needs these two tasks done.

CHAPTER SEVEN

Planting, hoeing, raking, shoveling (snow, mulch, dirt, gravel), planting, pruning trees and bushes.... The list of yardwork is virtually endless, and all of it is exercise to some degree. It's a lot more rewarding
if you also do at least some of the planning for it.

Hiking

"Hiking" often brings to mind a strenuous aerobic workout, climbing
up the side of a mountain with a pack strapped to your back as you
spend hours or days following a rough trail. It can be that. But it can
also be following a far gentler, and shorter, trail through the woods
near your home, enjoying the cooler air under the leafy canopy on a
warm summer day. You decide what you can comfortably handle.

Some activities are easy to do alone, but hiking tends to be a group
activity because it is easy to become lost or injured on a hike. Even a
twisted ankle on a short one mile hike can be a real problem. Would
you want to walk/hobble for a half mile on a sprained ankle with no
help? I know I wouldn't!

If your family doesn't already hike, see if you can get them interested
or gather a group of friends to go hiking. Start out with a short hike
near home and gradually increase your hiking range and difficulty as
you improve. Stop when it gets as hard as you want, or its taking too
much time.

In most areas, the hardest part of finding a trail isn't finding *one*, it is
narrowing down the choices to just one to start with. Parks and rec-
reation departments from the local level all the way up through the

PHYSICAL FITNESS

National Park Service build and maintain hiking trails. Even many housing developments have them.

Choices range from short, flat walking trails that even a senior citizen with a walker could handle to the Appalachian Trail, which runs from Maine to Georgia and includes some truly challenging sections. Some are educational include lessons local or national history, plants, and animals. Others have themes, such as watching birds or butterflies.

The goal is being physically fit. **If you and your group don't enjoy the activity, you won't stick with it.** If the trails are too easy (or you do the same ones too often), it gets boring. If they are too hard, it gets frustrating. If they take too much time from other activities (too hard or too long), then it adds to your stress instead of helping lower it.

Do hikes that work for you and your group. As you hike more, you will (hopefully) have fun, build muscle memory, and develop good hiking habits.

So what does this have to do with survival skills? If you have a car accident, get stuck, run out of gas, etc., you may have to hike out for help, and you probably don't want to walk in the middle of the road, even if it seems deserted. It just takes one crazy fast driver zooming out of nowhere to end a human life. That leaves you hiking on the side of the road. Even if it is mere feet to a smooth asphalt surface, you'll be safer if you are used to compensating for bumpy terrain, avoiding boggy bits, and navigating around hills and boulders.

CHAPTER SEVEN

Martial Arts

There are tons of different martial arts to choose from. Some, like Tai Chi, are really not very good for self-defense, but they do help with becoming and remaining calm—an important ability when things go badly. Martial arts remain one of the best, and best-known, forms of self-defense. They are also an outstanding form of physical fitness. (Self-defense is discussed more in Book 3 of this series, *26 Mental and Urban Life Skills*.)

There are a few factors that go into deciding which one to study. The first and most obvious ones are whether there is a dojo/studio to study at near you and how expensive it is. Next, consider the quality of instruction and the reputation of that studio. Finally, look at how well it suits you personally.

Learning a martial art requires going to class a minimum of 2-3 times per week. If there is no studio close enough for you to get to 2-3 times per week, keeping in mind your normal schedule, then you need to choose another style that does have a dojo near you.

Likewise, if the studio is too expensive for your family, including *all* the fees, then it is best to simply choose another style. Some styles have a large number of fees for belt tests and other studio events. If your family can afford classes but not belt fees, then it will be very difficult for you to advance because you cannot test and move on to harder classes. Choose another style to study, or possibly find a way to earn enough money yourself to pay for it.

Studio reputation matters because it can give you a good idea if it is strict, nurturing, youth-focused, adult-focused, etc. even better than a visit or advertising materials can. The simple truth is that some gyms and dojos really aren't nice to anyone who isn't a physically fit adult. Others aren't nice to anyone who isn't rich. Others aren't nice to anyone: they take a "tough-love" approach. That works for some people but not all of them. Most gyms are open and accepting to all who truly want to learn.

Take the time to listen to what people say about the dojo. Most are perfectly nice places and will treat you well, but it is worth the small amount of time to listen before you sign up.

Watching the actual instructor you will have teach a class and then taking a free intro class (most offer them) is also worth the time. If the instructor makes you uncomfortable or you can't understand their teaching style, look for another dojo. It isn't the right place for you The simple fact is that different people learn different ways. **An incredible instructor for one person can be an utter fail for another because they simply don't learn the same way.**

Swimming in Natural Bodies of Water

Swimming in a natural body of water—a lake or pond or ocean—isn't the same as swimming in a pool. The water moves all by itself, and there is stuff in it. If you are or often are near the ocean, everyone in the family should learn about currents, rip tides, and how to stay safe in the ocean (Book 3 of this series: *Outdoor Life Skills*).

If you have only ever swum in a chlorinated pool and never in a natural body of water, it can be an unsettling experience. The water isn't clear, it might smell weird, there is stuff floating in it, and there is probably stuff brushing up against your legs and crunching under foot. Taking all that in could be enough to make anyone freeze up while they absorb all the differences. Freezing up in an emergency is bad, especially if you are in water over your head and must swim.

Being dropped into water over your head in an emergency is unlikely, but so are most emergencies. And this is an excuse to go to the beach (lake, river, whatever) and go swimming. Use the excuse and give it a try!

Activity

Do an online search for "martial arts" and your town name to see what's available near you. Do any sound interesting? Search online and read about some of the styles available near you, especially the studios that sounded interesting.

Talk with your family and friends about what sounds fun, and not so fun, about each one. Most studios offer at least one free lesson. Talk to your parents or guardian about trying one, for free.

Quick Quiz

T/F   Swimming in a pool is exactly like swimming in the ocean, a lake, or a river.

T/F   Hiking can be a fun family activity.

T/F   There are only a few possible types of exercises.

T/F   Chores can be a good way to get exercise.

T/F   All martial arts are the same.

Resources

Note: Resources for Swimming are included in Chapter 22.

Articles

Getting Started in Biking
http://bicycling.about.com/od/howtoride/a/getting_started.htm

*The Hiker Mama
http://www.thehikermama.com/blog/2011/06/28/getting-started-hiking-with-kids/

Hiking Basics: Getting Started with Hiking
http://www.abc-of-hiking.com/hiking-basics/

How to Choose the Best Martial Arts for Kids
http://martialartslab.com/best-martial-arts-for-kids/

*How to Choose the Best Martial Arts School for Your Child
http://www.selfgrowth.com/articles/How_To_Choose_The_Best_Martial_Arts_School_F
or_Your_Child.html

*REI: Getting into Bicycling
http://www.rei.com/learn/expert-advice/getting-into-biking.html

Riding Tips: Getting Started
http://www.ridemybike.com/info/tips/gettingstarted

Trail Dames_(Hiking group for women)
http://www.traildames.com/index.html

Books

The Bicycling Big Book of Cycling for Beginners: Everything a New Cyclist Needs to Know to Gear Up and Start Riding by Tori Bortman

Bicycling for Fitness (Nutrition and Fitness for Teens) by Gustav Mark Gedatus

Complete Beginner's Guide to Picking a Martial Art by Chad Kunego

Essential Hiking for Teens (Outdoor Life) by Kristine Hooks

Kids' Easy Bike Care: Tune-Ups, Tools & Quick Fixes (Quick Starts for Kids!) by Steve Cole

Trekking on a Trail by Linda White

Scouting-Specific

Athletics Merit Badge
http://meritbadge.org/wiki/index.php/Athletics

Cross-Training Badge
http://forgirls.girlscouts.org/home/badgeexplorer/#cross-training

Cycling Merit Badge
http://meritbadge.org/wiki/index.php/Cycling

Hiking Merit Badge
http://meritbadge.org/wiki/index.php/Hiking

Locavore Badge
http://forgirls.girlscouts.org/home/badgeexplorer/#locavore

Physical Fitness Merit Badge
http://meritbadge.org/wiki/index.php/Personal_Fitness

PHYSICAL FITNESS

Practice with a Purpose Badge
http://forgirls.girlscouts.org/home/badgeexplorer/#practice-with-purpose

Sports Merit Badge
http://meritbadge.org/wiki/index.php/Sports

Staying Fit
http://forgirls.girlscouts.org/home/badgeexplorer/#staying-fit

Swimming Merit Badge
http://meritbadge.org/wiki/index.php/Swimming

Videos

7 Mistakes to Avoid When Choosing A Martial Arts School in Keller

(one is how well they clean the dojo)
https://www.youtube.com/watch?v=sHRRMWb9VVU

Bike Safety: How to Fit Kids for a Bike Helmets
https://www.youtube.com/watch?v=7afDZBatcVE

How to Perform a Basic Bike Fit
https://www.youtube.com/watch?v=1VYhyppWTDc

How to Properly Size and Fit a Bike for Kids
https://www.youtube.com/watch?v=aoUoNG2R0t4

Martial Arts Tips: How to Choose a Martial Art to Learn
https://www.youtube.com/watch?v=osLdP29jefw

{Part 2}
Food and Water

It's pretty simple: without enough healthy food and safe drinking water, we die.

Potable water. That means drinking water. If it's potable, it's safe for a person to ingest. You really can't assume water you find in puddle, stream, spring, etc. is safe to drink so filtering/purifying water is a critical skill to master.

A lot of people know you can add bleach to water to make it safe, but obviously drinking straight bleach is deadly. Knowing how much to add is critical. Likewise, knowing how to actually filter and purify water using other methods is extremely important. Even just knowing how filtering and purifying is different matters.

Other uses for water. We use many gallons of water per person every day in the USA, but very little of that needs to be potable. Cleaning and sanitation needs are the most obvious for non-potable water, but these aren't the only other ways we can use it in an emergency.

A lot of non-potable water can be reused even when there isn't an emergency. Practicing re-using water in a non-emergency will lower your water bills/well usage while helping the environment, and hopefully you will learn some good new habits. (Make sure to check local laws first.)

Grow your own food. This is admittedly a long-term project, but it is a great one even when there isn't an emergency. What better way to have fresh herbs and veggies than to have a window box or garden full of them?

Better yet: Since you are planting them, you get to grow the ones you like best, and skip the ones you hate. There is also the chance to grow something unusual, like carrots that aren't orange. Have some fun with it!

Preserve food. After Hurricane Sandy, many tons of food was thrown out because refrigerators stopped working and no one knew how to preserve their food, so it simply spoiled. In a disaster of that magnitude, a lot of waste is fairly inevitable, but if more people had known simple methods of preserving food like brining it, or if they had simply cooked the food that goes bad first, much more could have been salvaged and used.

Brining, dehydrating, canning, and freeze drying are all popular methods of preserving food. Not all of them (particularly freeze drying) are realistic for home use, but people have preserved food for lean times, including winter, through all of human history. Many are tried and true, and reasonably easy to do at home.

{Eight}

Potable (Drinking) Water

Having safe water is critical for survival. Finding water can be the difference between life and death. So can identifying if it's safe to drink, and knowing how to purify it since the short answer is that you can't ever assume it is safe to drink "found" water without treating it first.

Is it Safe to Drink?

Did you purify it? **It's only safe to drink if it's from a tap or bottle, or you purified it**—and sometimes tap water isn't potable either, but there are usually news stories when that happens. You need potable water any time it will enter your body, including ice cubes and brushing your teeth. Sometimes even tap water needs treated, but it's usually on the news when that happens.

Finding Water

Depending on where you are, you have different options. Your car may have a partial case of bottled water. You house may have 20 gallon jugs to use with a dispenser. Or you may be in a desert with no water in sight.

If it's raining, look for a container to catch the water. The water will be as clean as the air it falls through and the container you collect it. If the air is clear and the container is clean, the water will be relatively clean. If the air is full of ash or smog, that will contaminate the water. If there is residue left in the container from something else, it will end up in the water.

If you use a container that held frosting, expect the water to be sugary sweet and to taste like frosting. If it held oil.... Do you think you should *ever* drink water that was in a container with motor oil or other chemicals? Hopefully you said no, because that's a *big* no.

No matter what was in the container, I would still purify it because there could be contaminants in the air that are now in the water. I lived in LA for many years and the sky was always cleaner after it rained. The rain brought all that ick down out of the sky with it. Rain water simply isn't always as clean as we want to believe it is.

If it's snowing or there is snow or ice around, melt that before you drink it. **If you drink/eat snow or ice, it's so cold that it can lower your internal body temperature if you don't melt it first.** That's very, very bad. It's so bad, it can kill, and that's no joke or exaggeration.

Sometimes you are near a big source of fresh water such as a pond, lake, stream, or river. This water may be safe, but it is unlikely. Animals die and rot away in the water. They use it for a bathroom. People dump things in, possibly upstream of you. There is no way to know what is in that water, so purify it before drinking any.

You might be near a source of salt water such as the ocean or certain big inland lakes. Salt water will do you no good in the search for potable water. There are ways to make it drinkable, but it will probably be faster in the long run to simply find a source of fresh water.

Filtering vs. Purifying

Filtering removes bits of things, like sand or bugs. It removes big particles, not small ones like bacteria. Purifying removes or kills germs and bacteria, although some methods are more effective than others. Filtering first and then purifying is the best practice for drinking water, in part because it extends the life of your purifier and in part because some purification methods (such as boiling) do absolutely nothing to filter out debris.

Making it Drinkable

There are many ways to purify water. Some are faster, some are cheaper, and some are easier. Your best bet is to know how to use more than one method in case you can't use your favorite method for some reason.

Bleach

Adding household bleach (5.25% to 8.25% chlorine) to water is one of the more well-known ways to kill the germs and bacteria in water.

It is not safe to use bleach with added ingredients such as colors or scents. Bleach does not remove bits and pieces of debris or dirt, so water definitely needs to be filtered before adding the bleach.

Put the water into a clean container. Add five drops of bleach per liter or quart of water and mix well. Although this method kills many bacteria and viruses, it doesn't kill all of them.

Be aware that bleach does expire. Once it expires after about six months, it becomes progressively less effective until it is eventually totally useless.

Boiling and Pasteurization

Boiling has long been a standard way to kill germs and bacteria. It still works, but pasteurization has been discovered to work as well.

You know how school lunch milk says it is "homogenized, pasteurized" milk? Pasteurization happens at an almost, but not quite, boiling temperature that kills germs and bacteria.

For milk, that means it isn't ruined by being boiled. In a survival situation, it means your water is drinkable slightly faster, will cool to a drinkable temperature sooner, and you need to devote less time and firewood to it. However, it can be hard to know when you reach that temperature without expensive commercial equipment. That's where the WAPI enters the picture.

A WAPI (Water Pasteurization Indicator) is a small glass vial on a string. It has wax in it that melts when the water around it reaches pasteurization temperature. The wax slides down into the other end of the vial when your water (or milk) is safe to drink.

Small, cheap (about $7), easy to use, and infinitely reusable (as long as it doesn't break): I love the WAPI.

Filtering

It is possible to make a simple filter with the most rudimentary tools. You need two containers, one that only holds filtered water and one that only holds unfiltered water. If you don't, the filtered water will be re-contaminated. Put small holes in he bottom of the unfiltered container so the water, but not the filtering material, can drip through into the clean container.

Lots of materials can be used as the "filtering material" but layering charcoal (from a fire), cotton, and gravel is probably the most common method. Start with the material that will catch the largest pieces at the top, then smaller pieces, then the smallest. This usually works out to be a t-shirt or coffee filter on the bottom to remove the smallest particles. Sand or finely crushed charcoal is placed above that for slightly larger particles, with gravel/rocks on top. It is also possible to use the stuffing from a pillow as the bottom layer, instead of a t-shirt or coffee filter.

Boiling or other purification is still required after filtering.

Purification Systems

There really are some amazing systems available at very reasonable prices today. Many cost less than $20, and even the largest are less than $300. The price of water bottles with integrated filters is $30-$40 for each brand mentioned below. Each of these brands simply requires the water to be poured in and the filter does all the work as the water passes through.

Berkeys use a long-life filter to remove submicron viruses and heavy metals. They are available from the 1.5 gallon Travel Berkey (for 1 - 3 people) up to the 6 gallon Crown Berkey (for 6-12+ people). Berkeys are more expensive for the simple reason that they are generally larger capacity and very solid. Their solidity is undoubtedly one reason that several of their models are primarily for "indoor" use. They aren't light-weight.

The **LifeStraw** is amazingly simple to use, and a very affordable choice. It removes bacteria and pathogens, but not viruses, so water that may have viruses should also be treated with tablets if human or animal waste products are suspected in the water. There is a larger family version that filters out viruses, but the individual use version is far more common.

The LifeStraw is widely used, by anyone who can get one, in third world countries. It doesn't remove either heavy metals or salt, but it remains an outstanding choice for easy to use individual water purification needs.

Per their website, **Sawyer** water filters and purifiers "are certified for ABSOLUTE microns making it impossible for harmful bacteria, protozoa, or cysts like E. coli, Giardia, Vibrio cholera and Salmonella typhi (which cause Cholera and Typhoid) to pass through."

Sawyer has products for groups as well as micro filters for individuals. Their flagship filter is a simple, light-weight pouch designed to be rolled or squeezed to create a faster flow rate for drinking. Fill, squeeze, and drink.

Camelback systems have become increasingly popular and the filtration/purification market has not neglected them. (Camelbacks have a bladder filled with water the user carries on their back; a straw attached to the bag allows the user to drink from it while they are walking.) Sawyer, in particular, has an option that works with camelbacks. Simply fill it with unclean water and attach the filter. The water will be purified before it is drunk.

Solar Stills

Solar distilling is usually the final option to try because it is extremely slow, but it does work for even the dirtiest water and requires few resources.

Put the water in a bowl. Put a second (empty) bowl in the middle and cover with plastic, even a plastic bag will do. Lay something small in the center so the bag is held just a little lower over the empty bowl. As it heats up outside, the water will evaporate and condense on the underside of the plastic. The small center weight will make all the drips roll toward it and eventually drip into the bowl in the center. The dirt and impurities are left in the original bowl.

POTABLE (DRINKING) WATER

Tablets

Possibly the most commonly used option is water purification tablets. Widely available, easy to use, cheap, and effective, they should be part of every emergency bag. Since they run out fairly quickly, having a second system is more of a requirement than an option for any but a truly short emergency.

A best practice might be to use a purification system, such as the ones discussed above, for the majority of water and reserve tablets for truly suspect water. Double- (or triple-) treating water that may have sewage contamination is never, ever a bad idea.

Transpiration

In a true emergency situation with no other options readily available, there is something called "transpiration." The short version is that plants perspire, too, but they "sweat out" water we can drink reasonably safely, as long as the plant isn't poisonous (like poison ivy).

For transpiration, secure a plastic bag (grocery bag, freezer bag—whatever you have with you) around a bunch of green leaves on a non-poisonous plant, even an evergreen like a Christmas tree. The longer the bag is in the sun, the faster/more water you will harvest. When you are finished, tip the bag so the water pools in a corner and either make a hole in the corner to drink out of or open the bag and pour the contents into a something else to drink out of.

UV Filters

UV purifying systems, such as the SteriPen, kill microbes, pathogens, germs, and waterborne illnesses such as cholera. The UV light disrupts the DNA of microbes within seconds so they can't reproduce or make you sick.

Activity

Find a purification method you like. Go to a stream near you and fill a bottle with water. Try to get it from an area that is fairly clear. If the water isn't fairly clear when you look at the bottle, filter it filter it until it is. You may need to do it more than once.

When the water looks reasonably clear, purify and drink it.

Quick Quiz

T/F   UV light filters make bacteria multiply, leaving your water more unsafe for drinking

T/F   There is one best way to purify water for drinking

T/F   Boiling water is not a good way to filter it.

T/F   Water filters/purifiers always take a lot of space.

T/F   Filtering and purifying mean the same thing.

POTABLE (DRINKING) WATER

Resources

Articles

7 Tips for Finding Natural Sources of Water
http://thesurvivalmom.com/finding-natural-sources-of-water/

Purify Water with Bleach
http://www.doh.wa.gov/Emergencies/EmergencyPreparednessandResponse/Factsheets/
WaterPurification

WAPI
http://solarcooking.wikia.com/wiki/Water_Pasteurization_Indicator

What is Potable Water?
http://www.wisegeek.com/what-is-potable-water.htm

Books

SHTF Preparedness. Water Purification & Filtration by Chris Brooks
(SHTF = Stuff Hits the Fan) (Family Project)

Water 4 Survival (A Wilderness Survival Topic Book 3) by Paul Andrulis

The Water Collection Handbook - A Guide To Collecting, Treating, and Storing Water (Self Sustained Living) by Jonathon Toth (Family Project)

Other

Big Berkey (Travel Berkey)

LifeStraw (LifeStraw Water Bottle)

Sawyer Mini Water Filtration

SteriPen (UV Filter)

WAPI

Videos

Renovo Trio Emergency Filter Vs Sawyer Mini, LifeStraw, and Berkey Sport
https://www.youtube.com/watch?v=k4sBkR9eJzk

Kid Science: Make a Mini Water Filter
https://www.youtube.com/watch?v=RqWV7ozfFNQ

Solar Still on Ocean and Obtaining Food (Survival Zone)
https://www.youtube.com/watch?v=PP9D0M2nS0A

Survival Water Procurement: Transpiration Bag
https://www.youtube.com/watch?v=srOQuHxj_dU

Water Pasteurization Indicator (WAPI)
https://www.youtube.com/watch?v=rKsVcB_07iI

{Nine}

Other Uses for Water

Per the EPA: The average American family of four uses 400 gallons of water per day. On average, approximately 70 percent of that water is used indoors, with the bathroom being the largest consumer (a toilet alone can use 27 percent!).

The average African family uses 5 gallons. Why such a big difference? A lot of it boils down to, well, the need to boil. Americans have the luxury of having essentially unlimited, safe, clean water from multiple taps in their homes. Africans have to lug their water a long distance, then boil or otherwise treat it to make it safe to drink.

Since our water is so convenient, we use lots of it to clean all kinds of things, and for our toilets. When there is barely enough water for eating and drinking, no one is judged for wearing clothing more than once before washing it, even if it is mud-stained.

Gray water is water that isn't clean enough to drink, but isn't terribly dirty and often contains soap residue. Water from the washing machine is grey water. Local ordnances (laws) vary, but you may be able to use this grey water for many of the purposes discussed below. Other areas forbid it. Please make sure to check local laws before using gray water, especially in a non-emergency situation.

The point to remember is this: **not all water usage is equal.** Some requires scrupulously clean water, such as drinking water for a person with an immune problem. Some requires clean, pure water, such as drinking and eating. Many of our daily uses simply require clean water, free of dirt and debris. We can clean our bodies and our clothing perfectly well with water that might not be suitable for drinking. A few cleaning and outdoor uses, such as watering plants, do not even require clean water, although it shouldn't have any chemical residue.

By carefully choosing how clean the water really needs to be, it's not hard to reduce your water usage and how much time you need to spend finding, filtering, and purifying water in an emergency.

Cleaning

Washing your hands, washing your plate, washing your clothing…. We use a lot of water to wash things every day. Other than washing foods like vegetables and berries, and brushing teeth, most of our cleaning needs don't require potable water.

Before indoor plumbing, people simply wore and used things longer (when they were dirtier) than we do today. They also re-used water in ways it would never occur to most of us today. The same water might be used multiple times but there was a method to it. The more times it was used, the dirtier the task it was used for. (Makes sense.)

Once they pumped water and carried it to their home, people used the clean water for drinking and cooking needs first. Whatever was left, they used for cleaning whatever they thought needed to be cleanest or was least dirty to start with. That probably included church clothing and any utensils, plates or cups that were being washed, although it is unlikely that most were cleaned every day.

That same water, which we would consider dirty and unusable, was then used to clean other things. Perhaps counters and tables were washed down, or pots and pans scrubbed clean with it. Perhaps everyday clothing was washed. Whatever the choice, it wasn't simply tossed out.

This same water might be used *yet again* to do a first pass of cleaning on the dirtiest items, such as mud-spattered boots or clothing. More likely, the items would have been left to dry and most of the mud brushed, shaken, or otherwise knocked off first, if possible.

When the water was used for as many cleaning purposes as possible, it was time to pour it out but that doesn't mean it wasn't still getting one final use. It could still water the garden, rinse mud off the front walkway, or put out a fire.

If the water was used for a bath, then everyone in the family took a bath in the same water, starting with mom and dad and continuing down through the youngest baby. The story is that the water could end up so dirty that people might literally throw the baby out with the bathwater because they couldn't see it!

When any resource, including water, is scarce, being creative in finding the most possible ways to use it before declaring it waste/trash is important. It is surprising to you to read how many ways one container of water can be used?

Fire Safety

Camp and cooking fires are common in emergency situations where we don't have all the conveniences of home, like fire extinguishers and a nearby, on-call fire department. Depending on the situation, you may not be able to do much more than be careful of where you situate the fire, but it is still good to know your options.

In this situation, fill a 5 gallon or similar size bucket with water and keep it near the fire. If you don't have one of those, ask a local bakery to hold one for you or buy one at a hardware store. Even in the middle of the woods, there may be empty coffee or other cans (garbage) that can be used to hold some water to use on the fire but be sure the container isn't oily.

Using water that might, even possibly, have residue from oil, gas, or anything flammable to "put out" a fire could be very dangerous. Otherwise, it's just important to have water nearby in case a fire starts to get out of control, or sparks or a blown bit from the fire catch something on fire outside of the fire pit. It does not need to be potable at all since it isn't going anywhere near being put into a person's body.

When you are done with a fire, you need to be 110% certain it is entirely out and there are no live coals (embers) left in the fire pit. They can rekindle the fire later, after you have left or gone to sleep and there is no one nearby to keep it safe. If you use water to douse the fire completely, this lowers that risk a lot. Make sure to poke around, moving coals, logs, etc. to be sure nothing is glowing red or flaming. If it is, add more water until it isn't.

Gardening

The water is literally being poured onto and into dirt. Literally. How could having all the dirt removed possibly be a pre-requisite to adding it to the dirt?

As with fire safety, be aware of any contaminants that might cause a problem. If you are watering something you plan to eat, whether it's tomatoes, strawberries, or an apple tree, do not pour chemicals on top of them.

This is often a great use for gray water, but be sure to pour it onto dirt because the dirt may contain microorganisms that are effective against soap residue. Some rocks have lichen growing on them that the residue may damage.

Sanitation

This is covered in more detail later, but hopefully it's obvious why potable water isn't necessary for certain basic sanitation needs, like a latrine.

Activity

Make a list of all the ways you use water for one day. Include uses at home, like brushing your teeth and laundry, and out and about, such as going to the car wash or a water park. Include school, clubs, camps, and any other activities you go to.

Which ones require potable water and which do not? For the ones that don't require potable water, what other concerns might you have? What resources do you have to find, gather, or collect water?

Quick Quiz

T/F   We need potable water for everything in our daily life.

T/F   The average American uses under five gallons of water a day.

T/F   Water should never be re-used for a second task.

T/F   Contaminants (oil, pesticides) affect how you can use water.

T/F   Americans use more water for cleaning than many other countries.

Resources

Articles
American Water Usage
http://www.drinktap.org/home/water-information/conservation/water-use-statistics.aspx

Greywater Basics
http://oasisdesign.net/greywater/createanoasis/#basics

Indoor Water Use in the United States
http://www.epa.gov/watersense/pubs/indoor.html

Safe Use of Household Greywater
http://aces.nmsu.edu/pubs/_m/M106.html

Water Recycling
http://www.epa.gov/region9/water/recycling/

Water Usage Facts
http://www.waterinfo.org/resources/water-facts

Books

The Complete Guide to Water Storage: How to Use Gray Water and Rainwater Systems, Rain Barrels, Tanks, and Other Water Storage Techniques for Household and Emergency Use (Back to Basics Conserving) by Julie Fryer (Family Project)

Rainwater Harvesting for Drylands and Beyond, Volume 1, 2nd Edition: Guiding Principles to Welcome Rain into Your Life and Landscape by Brad Lancaster (Family Project)

Other

Rain Barrel (86 Gallon Collapsible Rain Barrel)

Rainwater Collection System Connector

{Ten}

Grow Your Own Food

No matter where you live, you can grow vegetables and herbs from seeds or seedlings, even in an apartment in a big city. You can even grow small trees or have a container garden.

It should go without saying, but don't spray any chemicals like insect repellants on plants you intend to eat. It's just not safe.

Fruit trees clearly take the longest time to show the fruits of your labor. Once they do, they can continue to do so for many years to come, with proper care, thus the expressions "bearing fruit" and "the fruit of your labors." Berries and dwarf trees take several years to produce much. Herbs can produce large amounts in mere months.

These are all generally perennials, although certain herbs may not be. That means once you plant them, they come back every year until they die or you rip them out and replace them with something different. Even then, some herbs may just grow back if there is even a small amount of root left. (Mint of all sorts is well-known for being almost impossible to eradicate once it gets established.)

Vegetables and grains, on the other hand, are annuals. You have to save (or buy) new seeds to plant every year. It is hard to imagine that it's a coincidence that the foods humans eat the most, and have cultivated the longest, now require the most human help to thrive.

The seeds for many plants are modified (GMO) for a specific reason like having better color, better flavor, blooming a certain time, surviving in a certain climate, and many more reasons. This often results in a plant that produces seeds that can't be used to plant a new crop for the next year, which means that you have to buy new seeds every year. Even if they do sprout, the seedlings from these plants tend to be less numerous and less healthy. That's not saying it is true for all modified seeds, but it is true for many.

Seeds that haven't been modified at all are called "heirloom seeds", which is not the same thing as organic, although many are both. Heirloom seeds are older seeds that haven't had any genetic modifications made to them. They produce plants where you can harvest the seeds and plant them to produce a good crop of healthy seedlings for the next year.

Berries

Strawberries were initially the easiest for me to grow, but died out almost entirely over two tough winters. Raspberries are my favorite, and golden raspberries are my absolute favorite. Yes, golden raspberries. It's almost impossible to find them unless you grown them yourself. It's the same for many other foods like purple (dragon) carrots.

Berries grow in different ways. A few grow close to the ground, like strawberries. Those grow quickly. Many berries grow on bushes, and bushes take time to grow. A few, like mulberries, even grow on trees, but most are on bushes.

When planting berry bushes, the most common (and by far easiest) way is to buy and plant a bush from a nursery. Choose a good location and take care of it, and in a few years you just may have a large crop of berries.

Flowers (Edible)

Yes, flowers are edible. People used to eat roses and violets as treats. Sugared violets were a particular treat in the late 1800s. Dandelions have long been known for having healing properties.

Today, many of us use pesticides to keep our flowers bug-free and pretty. Those can't be eaten, but if you make a commitment to not spraying them and to making sure no one else does, you can try them yourself. I don't think anyone will add these as a regular part of a modern diet, but it is kind of an interesting thing to do for something different, and to tell your friends.

In addition to dandelion, purple coneflower (Echinacea) and lavender are two examples of decorative plants that also have herbal healing properties. If you are interested in herbal healing, there are many others that can be eaten and used as medicine.

Fruit and Nuts

Once they are established, fruit and nut trees can last for decades, or even longer. They can produce a lot, or almost nothing. The biggest early mistake is only planting one or two trees when you need more for them to cross-pollinate and have healthy fruit.

Sometimes, the problem is beyond your control. The White House has an apple tree that stopped producing fruit for years. One year, bee hives were established nearby and it started producing again. The smallest things can have a huge impact.

Some fruits and a few berries won't produce fruit if you only have one. The nursery you buy them from can help you buy what you need to get the best yield.

Research what grows well in your area or just ask at a good nursery. If lots of people near you have almond or pear trees, it's safe to take that as proof they grow well in your area. If you want to grow something different, research it online first. The next step is talking to local nurseries to see what they recommend. They will know things books and websites can't tell you, such as whether local animals will steal all your fruit, there is a parasite that affects one particular crop, or even if a common plant in your area will kill it. (Deer eat everything, including plastic plants when truly desperate.)

Grains and Sprouts

Truthfully, this isn't something to plant in an apartment or small home. You really need a fairly large amount of land to grow enough grain to be useful, but it is an important part of our diets.

Sprouting seeds is, however, doable in even a very small space. Sprouting is simply getting a seed to germinate and start to grow, and then eating it either raw or cooked. Sprouts are extremely nutritious.

Herbs

Herbs can be very hardy and often grow wild. In my experience, they are the easiest part of my garden and the best smelling. They also survive the winter well. Oregano has done so well that I am moving it to be a border where nothing else will grow in the yard.

Many herbs are used in cooking and in traditional medicine, such as chamomile tea to help sleep. The herbs your family uses for these purposes are a good place to start.

Beware mint! Once planted, it grows and grows and can even take over a yard. Mint is best planted in a cement container to keep it confined, or possibly on an area like a creek bank that you want overgrown to prevent erosion but won't plant anything else on. I have planted mint in my garden, unaware it was in the mint family, and it's OK, but I do have to pull out a lot more random new shoots from that than from many other plants.

There are lots of plants in the mint family. Spearmint and peppermint are obvious, but bee balm and lemongrass are more of a surprise. The nursery staff can tell you which plants are in the mint family.

Veggies

Vegetables can be finicky to grow. People have tended them in gardens, watering them and giving them the best soil for so many centuries that they now demand it, or they don't do well. Since they are a basic and necessary part of our diet, it is worth the time spent.

My favorite heirloom seeds are for dragon carrots. They are a reddish-purple color, which I think is cool. When you grow your own food, you can find new varieties that no one around you has and have a lot of fun.

Activity

Look through seed catalogs and find berries, flowers, fruit, herbs, and veggies you like that grow in your growing zone. Think about where you would plant them in your yard and make a map showing your garden plan. Show your parents or guardians and see if you can actually do some or all of what you sketched out.

Quick Quiz

T/F   Herbs are often easier to grow than other plants.

T/F   Vegetables are often finicky to grow.

T/F   Fruit and nut trees take at least a decade or two to begin producing much.

T/F   Seed catalogs are a great place to find new plants.

T/F   It is not important to know your growing zone when shopping for plants and seeds.

Resources

Articles

Family Gardening
http://www.kidsgardening.org/family-gardening

Getting Started Sprouting
http://www.living-foods.com/articles/sprouting.html

Growing Berries
http://www.motherearthnews.com/organic-gardening/growing-berries-zl0z0905zhyd.aspx

Growing Fruit Trees in Containers
http://www.starkbros.com/blog/fruit-trees-in-containers-pt1/

*Herb Gardens for Children
http://www.gardeningknowhow.com/special/children/herb-gardens-for-children.htm

Kids Gardening
http://shop.kidsgardening.org/?

*Sprouting Seeds
http://sproutpeople.org/growing-sprouts/sprouting-basics/

Books

Container Gardening with Kids: 7 Easy Steps to Bountiful Harvests for Everyone by Mary Verdant

The Everything Sprouted Grains Book: A complete guide to the miracle of sprouted grains by Brandi Evans

Garden to Table: A Kid's Guide to Planting, Growing, and Preparing Food by Katherine Hengel

Roots, Shoots, Buckets & Boots: Gardening Together with Children by Sharon Lovejoy

Ultimate Book of Step-by-Step Cooking and Gardening Project for Kids by Nancy McDougal and Jenny Hendy

Other

Sprouting Seeds Sample Pack

Sprouting Tray

Scouting-Specific

Gardening Merit Badge
http://meritbadge.org/wiki/index.php/Gardening

Plant Science Merit Badge
http://meritbadge.org/wiki/index.php/Plant_Science

Videos

[Time Lapse] Mung Bean Germination
https://www.youtube.com/watch?v=pB4ASdELBbQ

Time lapse radish seeds sprouting, top and roots growing
https://www.youtube.com/watch?v=d26AhcKeEbE

{Eleven}

Preserve Food

There are lots of ways to preserve food at home, and many of them are super easy. Brining and making jerky have been done for thousands of years. Because it is impossible to know you have killed all the bacteria in home preservation, the food doesn't usually stay good for nearly as long as professionally processed foods, although canned goods are usually safe for quite a few years.

Big companies use modern, high-tech methods to produce the dehydrated, powdered, and freeze-dried long-term storage food available at the grocery store and online. Because of the automated systems used, they are able to ensure a higher percentage of water is removed from dehydrated and freeze dried food, thus ensuring it will stay safe to use for decades instead of months or years.

Dehydrating, smoking, and creating jerky all use heat to remove all the water from the food. The end result is tougher, smaller, and crunchier food. Brining and canning use water, resulting in food that looks more like fresh food.

Brining

This is the process of preserving food in salt water and is one of the oldest known methods for preserving food. Home-brined food may stay good for 6-12 months, if it is kept cool, but this isn't a method for storing food for decades. While you can brine any kind of meat, it is most effective for poultry and pork. It doesn't do much for beef.

In brining, the salt water enters all the spaces in the meat, which prevents oxygen from doing the same. Oxygen makes food spoil, so this keeps it from going bad, but, as with so many things, it needs to stay below 40°F or so for maximum freshness. As the salt penetrates the meat, it brings along any other spices mixed in with it, making brining a great way to add flavor to your food.

In modern usage, brining is primarily done to flavor the meat. As such, most online recipes use much less salt than is needed for long-term storage.

Most Americans are more than familiar with the blue canisters synonymous with table salt, but that doesn't make it the best choice for everything salty. Kosher, pickling, and table salt, but *not* sea salt, are recommended for brining.

The brining process is fairly simple: submerge the meat in a solution of salt and water. Make sure it stays fully covered until you are ready to eat it. You need approximately 1 cup of salt for every gallon of cold water.

Meat has a tendency to float in the water, so use some sort of weight to hold it down. A brick or paperweight in a zippered baggie will do, just make sure it's not an open baggie that will let dirt and germs from the item into the brining and your meat. Pie crust weights work as well.

If you are storing the meat for a few weeks or months (not just flavoring it), it will need several inches of water at the top and shouldn't be kept in a metal container because the metal may rust or make food taste metallic. Plastic isn't a great choice either. (Think about how water tastes in a plastic bottle after a few hours, now imagine after a few months.) Cover and store in a cool place.

The links in the Resource section of this chapter provide more how-to specifics.

Canning

Home canned goods are healthier than comparable manufactured goods. You control what goes—and doesn't go—into your food.

You don't like onions? Good luck finding a manufactured salsa without them (trust me, I've tried), but if you make your own, that problem is solved. The same goes for virtually every other food.

Canning is its own section in many "Cookbooks" areas at bookstores, so I am simply providing a few books and supplies in the Resources section for anyone interested in learning how to can.

Dehydrating

Simply put, dehydrated food has had the water removed using relatively low levels of heat (150-200°F or so versus 350°F+ to cook) to extend how long it is safe to eat. Food pieces shrink to just a fraction of their original size and need rehydrated before being used in most recipes. Once rehydrated, most look very similar to fresh.

Dehydrated may sound a bit odd, but most of us have cooked with dehydrated food because most of us have, at some point, eaten Kraft Mac 'n' Cheese™, and that includes dehydrated cheese and pasta. Most of us have also, at some point, had box-mix potatoes or stuffing. Why do you think they fluff up so much when you add water or milk? Because they are dehydrated!

Personally, I have kept instant (dehydrated) milk at home since I discovered it in college. While I have no intention of drinking the stuff, it's great for baking when I run out of fresh milk.

Jerky

Jerky is dehydrated strips of meat with the fat and water removed. It is usually marinated in spices before being jerked. Originally, it was smoked or salted along with being jerked to ensure it would last for more than a couple of weeks. Even without any further processing, two weeks is longer than most meat will last in the refrigerator.

Smoking

Smoking is the very old process of using a fire to remove water from meat so it can be stored for a much longer time. Smoked meat has a different flavor because it absorbs the smoke during the long time it is being smoked.

Meat must be fresh and thawed, and salt should not contain added iodine ("iodized").

Cheese can also be smoked, but fruits and veggies are not normally smoked.

Activity

If you can, try preserving food using one of these techniques. If not, try this with store-bought food.

Pick one food you like. Try it several different ways, including fresh. If you like corn, try fresh corn, canned corn, and dehydrated corn. If you like beef, try a fresh burger, a dehydrated burger (available from companies like Mountain House), beef jerky, and canned beef (near the canned tuna in the grocery store).

Which one(s) do you like and not like? How are they different? Which, if any, do you want to add any to your regular diet or emergency supplies?

Quick Quiz

T/F   You can preserve food for long-term storage (1-2 years) at home.

T/F   Professional companies can prepare food so it is good for 20 years or longer.

T/F   Fruits and veggies are often smoked.

T/F   Brining is a modern technique for preserving food.

T/F   Dehydrating is effective for nearly any kind of food

Resources

Use discretion when choosing how early to teach children how to use sharp, hot, or otherwise potentially dangerous items.

Articles

The Basics of Brining
http://momprepares.com/preserving-meat-the-basics-of-brining/2/

Preserving Meats: Salting and Brining
http://www.almanac.com/content/preserving-meats-salting-and-brining

Making Beef Jerky
http://www.wikihow.com/Make-Beef-Jerky

Smoking Meat
http://www.smoking-meat.com/

Internal Temps for Smoking Meat
http://nchfp.uga.edu/publications/nchfp/lit_rev/cure_smoke_pres.html

Books

The Ball Complete Book of Home Canning

Canning for a New Generation: Bold, Fresh Flavors for the Modern Pantry by Liana Krissoff

Food Storage: Preserving Vegetables, Grains, and Beans: Canning - Dehydrating - Freezing - Brining - Salting - Sugaring - Smoking - Pickling - Fermenting by Susan Gregersen

The Great American Jerky Cookbook: A simple guide to making your own authentic beef jerky by Amanda Stock

Meat Smoking And Smokehouse Design by Stanley Marianski

Smoking Food: A Beginner's Guide by Chris Dubbs

Ultimate Dehydrator Cookbook, The: The Complete Guide to Drying Food, Plus 398 Recipes, Including Making Jerky, Fruit Leather & Just-Add-Water Meals by Tammy Gangloff

Other

21.5 Quart Granite Wear Water Bath Canner

6 Piece Canning Set, Norpro (vital accessories only, no canner)

Canning Jars

Canning Lids

Canning Rings

Dehydrator (Nesco)

Dehydrator trays (small foods)

Dehydrator trays (liquefied, pureed foods)

COOKING AND CLEANING

Enamel Ware 9 Piece Canning Kit

Jerky Spices

{Part 3}
Cooking and Cleaning

Cooking is one of the most basic, and ancient, skills humans mastered. Without food, people die. Without safe food, they get sick and may die. Without tasty food, they get cranky and unhappy. Without the ability to cook and bake, they are dependent on others for this most basic need to be fulfilled, just like a baby.

At this point, you may be thinking that people used to just gather food and eat it. The truth is that there are very few foods that can be eaten without some kind of preparation. Berries, vegetables, and fruits can, but only when they are in season. A person who can't cook has to either live somewhere food can be grown year-round or they risk starving to death in the winter.

Safety Note: If there is a grease fire, turn off the heat and cover it with a metal (not glass) lid. A large amount of baking soda can extinguish a grease fire, but ***water does not put out grease fires.***

Staying clean may not be the oldest skill, but it is certainly one we all know is important. Hygiene and proper sanitation matter. Poor hygiene and sanitation kills more people than guns, and always has. In war, historically, infections and diseases caused by poor hygiene have been the top causes of death for soldiers, not actual battle-field injuries. In a disaster, much of what we take for granted (including medicine)may not be available, making this even more important.

Meal Planning: This is the part of cooking that sounds like the least fun, but can be the most fun. It's picking out the meals everyone in the family will eat for the next week or two, or whatever time frame is set. The person doing the meal planning can make certain there are no meals they dislike on the menu. Win!

Most families have a collection of (mostly unused) cookbooks. The internet also has many, many websites full of recipes. It is impossible to *not* find something mouthwatering looking through cookbooks or cooking websites! Choose things that look and sound yummy to you. Have fun with it!

Food Safety: No one likes being sick, but eating unsafe food is the fast track to illness. How ill depends on how spoiled the food is and the bacteria that contaminated it. Keeping food safe isn't terribly complicated (keep it at the right temperature and use promptly), but it's important to learn how to do that and what clues indicate food is spoiling/has spoiled.

Follow a Recipe: If you can't follow a recipe, you'll have a hard time learning how to cook, and an even harder one learning to bake. It really is that simple.

Hygiene and Sanitation: Having a reasonably clean body and maintaining a sanitary environment may be the most critical elements in staying alive long-term. **In war, more soldiers have died of disease**

than directly from battlefield injuries due to poor hygiene and sanitation. Understanding this is *important.*

It is also important to remember people don't like being around those with poor hygiene because they often smell bad. No one wants to be known as smelly, and it's a description that tends to hang around for a very long time, once someone is stuck with it.

Cleaning: Most people don't enjoy cleaning, but at least it has a clearly visible end result. Like many things, getting everything spit-spot can be a lot of work. To keep from having to make that big effort again, take a few minutes every day to put everything away. That includes unpacking when you return from a trip, even an overnight one, and putting away clean laundry.

Cleaning is critical for keeping critters and bugs away and having a safe, disease-free environment. If you can't clean up after yourself, you will end up with roaches, rats, mice, and more infesting your space. Once they arrive, it is very difficult (and potentially costly) to get rid of them.

The teen years are infamous for being messy, but the simple truth is that if your things have a place and you regularly put them there (in other words, put them away), it's easier to find them. A messy space makes it harder to find things, and easier to accidentally damage them. When you want to wear a certain thing (underwear, perhaps), it will immediately be clear if it is clean or not–*if* you actually folded your laundry and put it away.

{Twelve}

Meal Planning

Meal planning sounds like no fun until you realize that whoever plans the meals gets to make sure everyone is eating what that person likes, or at least doesn't hate.

No one likes eating the same thing over, and over, and over, so at the very least, you need seven choices each for breakfast, lunch, dinner, and a healthy snack. That gives you a full week of choices. Ideally, you'll do fourteen for each, giving you a two week menu and more time before you grow tired of each choice.

Most Americans have been taught about the five food groups using an FDA graphic showing how much we should eat of each food group everyday. It used to be the food pyramid, but changed to a newer pyramid, and then a plate with portions on it. No doubt it will change again, but whatever the image you are familiar with, the point is the same: we need a lot more of some food groups (fruits and vegetables) than others (sugars and fats).

The only realistic way to have a variety of food groups in our diet is to have a variety of foods. Soups, casseroles, and stir fries are each a good start for this. Having a truly balanced meal means eating side dishes along with a main course and having healthy snacks, but everyone already knows that. **Eating a well-balanced diet is much harder than knowing you need to, and that is where meal planning shines.**

Breakfast

It's the most important meal of the day. "Everyone" says so. If you are like a lot of people, it's really easy to sleep for an extra 10-15 minutes and just grab some kind of bar or other quick snack instead of a good breakfast. With a little planning, it's easy to have fast, nutritious breakfasts every day, or nearly every day.

Smoothies can be a healthy, fast breakfast, as long as you don't use a lot of ice cream and sugar in them. Having ground up ice cubes or plain yogurt is much healthier than adding ice cream and gives you a better start to your day.

Lunch

Most of us need a lunch we can carry to school, work, or camp. Sandwiches are the fastest, easiest choice, especially if you don't have a microwave to use. It's easy for that to become boring, but it doesn't have to.

Think about your favorite foods and how they can be turned into something different for lunch. My boys love Nutella. They also love marshmallows. Sometimes, they have sandwiches with Nutella and marshmallow fluff. It's like a s'mores sandwich. Dinner leftovers can make great lunches. Using turkey or chicken from dinner in a sandwich for lunch is a classic.

If you like simple sandwiches like turkey and cheese, adding condiments like spicy ketchup or honey mustard, or heating it to make a panini will give you a whole new sandwich experience. Even simple changes like buying a different cheese or meat (smoked turkey instead of oven baked) can be a big change.

Dinner

This is the biggest meal of the day for most families, and there are seemingly infinite choices. Most families have a few favorites they eat over and over again. You can include those meals, but you might try switching them up a bit or going from pre-packaged to homemade.

Many people eat grilled cheese with sliced, processed American cheese. Have you tried it with a different cheese, like cheddar or Swiss? Have you added tomatoes or bacon—even bacon bits? There are tons of ways to take a simple meal like grilled cheese and make it just a little bit different. Lots of foods can be similarly updated.

One meal we eat at least once a month is frozen fish and chips. My goal is to switch from frozen fish and chips to homemade, using panko breading. Panko is an Asian breading that is much lighter and less unhealthy.

Another meal we eat is frozen gyoza, a kind of Asian dumplings that

I no longer like. They changed the filling. I tried once, and will try again, to make them at home. With inexpensive store-bought wrappers, it was surprisingly easy.

Side Dishes

It's incredibly easy to just skip over the side dishes, but they are important. They can make a meal well-balanced and healthy, or not.

Veggies are an important side dish. It's easy to say "I hate all veggies" but the reality is that there are sooo many out there that there have to be at least a few you like! Personally, I can't stand iceberg lettuce so I didn't eat salads for 30 years. Then I discovered spinach and baby spinach. I love eating salads with those!

Working together as a family, find new vegetables to try and try old vegetables in new ways. Some things that are just nasty one way are amazing prepared another way, or fresh. I'm not a huge fan of tomatoes, but I love sun-dried tomatoes and home-made salsa.

Dessert and Snacks

Dessert is normally sweeter than the rest of the meal, but that doesn't mean it has to be unhealthy. Berries can be a dessert. Strawberry shortcake is a very popular summer dessert. If you make homemade shortcake and don't drown it in sugar, it's actually *very* healthy.

Many of us need a good-sized snack to keep going at some point in the afternoon. A big piece (or three) of brownie tastes lovely and is totally OK to have as a snack sometimes, but not every day. A bowl of mandarin orange slices or a healthy smoothie, on the other hand, would be a great choice to have every day, especially if it doesn't have any sugary syrup or ice cream added.

Drinks

Water should be your first and most frequent choice. Soda should be your last and least frequent choice. "Should" is different from "will" or "is", but in an emergency, soda will quickly stop being a choice at all.

Coffee is an American staple and many of us have enough on hand to last for a week or two, if not much longer, at our normal rate of use. In the Civil War era, during the Great Depression, and during other hard times, chicory root has been used to create a coffee-substitute.

I have no research to back this up, but I suspect tea is the second-oldest drink for humans, after water. Tea includes boiled water with just about any kind of herb or flower in it. Rose hips can be used to make tea. Peppermint, chamomile, lemon balm, lavender, and tons of other herbs and flowers can be used to make herbal teas. Even honeysuckle blossoms! And, of course, tea can be used to make tea.

The biggest benefit to coffee and tea in an emergency is that the water is always boiled as part of making it, so you can be sure it is safe to drink. Many herbal teas are also useful for medicinal purposes.

When the Transcontinental Railroad was built after the Civil War, massive amounts of workers on the western section died of diseases, until they brought in Chinese laborers. The bosses thought they were somehow immune, but the truth was far simpler. They boiled their water when they made tea, so they killed most of the germs that felled the other workers.

Tea is a great drink in an emergency. The fact that it can be drunk hot, to warm you when it's cold, or cold, to cool you when it's hot, is an added bonus to the delicious taste. With all the varieties available, if you don't enjoy tea, you probably just haven't had the right one yet.

Activity

Plan healthy meals, including side dishes, for your family for at least three days, but preferably for a full week.

Quick Quiz

T/F   Breakfast isn't an important meal.

T/F   Proper meal planning helps ensure a healthy diet.

T/F   Drinks cannot be part of a healthy meal.

T/F   Side dishes play a key role in ensuring all the food groups are represented.

T/F   Dessert doesn't have to be unhealthy.

Resources

Articles

*Menu and Meal Planning Printables
http://www.nourishinteractive.com/nutrition-education-printables/category/16-printable-kids-healthy-menu-plans-daily-meal-planner-childrens-healthy-food-groups-balanced-meals+

Menu Planning
http://organizedhome.com/kitchen-tips/menu-planning-save-time-kitchen

Books

7-Day Menu Planner For Dummies by Susan Nicholson

Plan It, Don't Panic: Everything You Need to Successfully Create and Use a Meal Plan by Stephanie Langford

Meal Planner: Blank Meal Planner by Frances P Robinson

Other

Food Planner (app)

Magnetic Pad: What to Eat (Meal Planner)

Weekly Meal Planner

Scouting-Specific

Cooking Merit Badge
http://meritbadge.org/wiki/index.php/Cooking

Dinner Party Badge
http://forgirls.girlscouts.org/home/badgeexplorer/#dinner-party

New Cuisines Badge
http://forgirls.girlscouts.org/home/badgeexplorer/#new-cuisines

CHAPTER TWELVE

Videos

Meal Planning with Children
https://www.youtube.com/watch?v=myHuWAq4Pkw

Kids Can Cook, Episode 13- "Planning a Meal" Part 1
https://www.youtube.com/watch?v=doGU0Do9c_I

{Thirteen}

Food Safety

Food safety starts with food handling and continues through safely disposing of food waste. Composting is one way to safely dispose of food waste.

"Sell By" and "Use By" do not mean the same thing. Sell by is the date the store needs to sell a product by to ensure the buyer doesn't need to use it the same day they buy it. The "Use By" date is the date after which it is no longer certain to be safe to eat.

For some foods, such as a bag of flour or dried herbs, those dates can be considered recommendations. A very tiny number of foods, including sugar and salt, almost never expire. For others, particularly meat, poultry, and seafood, it should be viewed as more of a hard deadline that is not to be ignored. Expired products with yeast can also contain dangerous mold that may not be visible to the naked eye.

Crackers and rice might both seem like they should stay good for a very long time, but they are just two of the many foods that have enough oils in them to go rancid quickly. Rancid food smells nasty. **Any food that smells nasty is no longer good to eat.**

Food Handling

The most basic principals are that everything needs to be:

1. Clean.

2. Separate (to prevent cross-contamination).

3. At a safe temperature. Keep cold foods cold (below 40°F) and hot foods hot (above 140°F).

Wash everything, including your hands, before you start. Many things will be clean because they were washed after the last use, but some may need wiped clean again, particularly counters.

Once you use something for anything other than water, it is no longer clean. For some things, it doesn't matter too much because they don't tend to carry a lot of germs. If you are baking and use a measuring cup for flour, it is perfectly normal to also use it for sugar and other dry ingredients, and then wash it once everything is finished.

For others, particularly meat, poultry, seafood, and other once-living sources of protein, it is extremely important. Once any form of raw meat touches a surface, it is potentially contaminated and needs to be well cleaned (not just wiped down) before anything else touches it. In other words, don't cut up a raw chicken and then use the same (unwashed) cutting board to cut up the greens for a salad.

When you buy food, keep meat and eggs in separate bags. If you carry them in reusable bags, *wash the bags regularly*. Anytime any food gets onto a bag, it needs washed before you use it again. If you don't, the bags can become a source of contamination. When you get the food home and store it, continue to keep the meat and eggs in separate containers and clean up any spills from them quickly using soap or another cleansing product, not just water. This is especially important if the spill is blood or other fluids. When you prepare food, use different cutting boards for raw meat, produce, and cooked meat.

All of these steps are intended to reduce or eliminate cross-contamination. If you watch the scene from the TV show *Scrubs* listed in the Resources section (*My Cabbage*), you can see how easy it is to cross-contaminate things and pass germs around.

Both before and after cooking, it is very important to store food at a safe temperature so bacteria don't multiply to a dangerous level. When cooking food, it is important to make it hot enough to kill any bacteria that are there. The best practice is to use a meat thermometer to be sure the food was cooked thoroughly enough to kill all the bacteria. The recommended temperatures for different kinds of meat are in the FDA article *Safe Food Handling* in the Resources section.

Spoiled Food

Food that has "spoiled" is not necessarily dangerous to eat, although it also isn't a good idea to eat it. Bread with mold on it is "spoiled" and unpleasant to eat, but is not dangerous in the way that uncooked food or water contaminated with e-coli is.

While no one recommends eating food that is moldy or has gone "off", the reality is that many people all over the world are able to eat it and our ancestors regularly ate spoiled food. Sauces were invented to cover those nasty tastes and smells!

Mexico is infamous as a place where people from countries with purer water can't drink the water without getting sick. Clearly, their water is bacteria-laden. And yet, the locals are able to drink it and survive. This doesn't mean it's OK to drink and eat questionable food or drinks. It means that it is very unlikely to kill a healthy person, but it could certainly make you feel extremely miserable.

Slime, mold, bad smells (except for a few cheeses), and odd colors are all signs a food is spoiled or spoiling and shouldn't be eaten. If you pull out a package of shredded cheddar cheese or a round of brie and it smells like feet, toss the feet cheese immediately.

When handling any spoiled or potentially spoiled food, it is best to wear gloves to keep bacteria off your hands. When you finish disposing of it, thoroughly clean any surfaces the spoiled food came in contact with to kill any bacteria transferred onto those surfaces.

Canned Food

First and foremost, if the seal on the can is broken in any way, including leaking, bursting, or bulging, then the food is no longer safe to eat. A dented can may have damage to the lining and also may not be safe to eat. You are taking a very real chance if you do.

As spoilage bacteria and yeasts grow, they produce gases that increase the pressure inside the can. That pressure leads to broken seals, spurting liquids, leaks, and bursting.

Home canned food, in particular, may spurt when opened if it is spoiled. Since the container is glass, there may also be visible mold or bacteria growing inside it, possibly starting at the top and growing down. A top layer of scum, slime or mold may be visible, as may air bubbles.

Simple discoloration is not always a sign that food is no longer edible, but it usually indicates that it will at least be less tasty. If the color is truly off, however, and if it smells unappetizing, toss it.

Food safety is definitely one area where "better safe than sorry" is an adage to follow. When in doubt, throw it out.

Frozen and Refrigerated Food

Even if the power goes out, most food will stay safe for up to four hours, if the doors are kept closed most of the time. After that, it will start going bad. How quickly depends on the temperature inside the refrigerator, outside the fridge, how long/often the door was open since the power went out, and the food itself. The FDA has a chart detailing which foods need discarded first (see **Resources**).

The more often the door is opened, the more cold air escapes and the warmer the fridge is. If you normally set the fridge at 45°F, then it will naturally warm up faster than if it is normally set at 37°F. Shrimp will spoil before carrots. Food in the freezer will start thawing, but will remain edible as long as it stays cold.

CHAPTER THIRTEEN

Most of it is just common sense.

Freezer Burn

Freezer burn is what happens to food that loses some of its moisture in the freezer. It is still perfectly edible, but may not be quite as tasty. If it is bothersome, simply cut off the most freezer-burnt sections and use the rest.

Freezer burn happens when the water molecules in food gradually turn to ice crystals in the freezer. As they accumulate on the food, it may change color. This color change and loss of water inside the food is what we see as "freezer burn." It no longer looks as nice and doesn't taste quite as good, but it is still safe to eat.

Safe Disposal

It is important not to let spoiled and rotting food just set around. It creates a biohazard. Care needs to be taken in disposing of it the right way to keep everyone safe.

Composting

In terms of food waste, composting is primarily for leftover grains, fruits, and vegetables. It is not for meat, seafood, poultry, or eggs. (Cleaned out eggshells can be included.) Basically, if it was or could have been an animal, don't compost it. This green waste is mixed with brown waste (leaves, grass clippings, wood, straw, etc.). The starred Articles in the Resources section have more detailed information.

Mixing yard waste such as dead leaves or ash in every time you add food waste to your composter is a best practice. Critters may be drawn to your compost to search for anything that is still edible, particularly if you make the mistake of including any meat, seafood, poultry, or egg waste. Mixing your leftover food scraps with yard waste makes it less appealing, so the critters stay away.

There are some kinds of critters that are good to have in your compost. Worms are so good that certain kinds of composting–vermiculture–require them. Soldier fly larvae sound gross, but do an outstanding job of helping the composting process along.

Eventually, compost is added to the garden as new soil. Anything and everything you put in the compost is part of that soil. If you put weeds in your compost, any surviving seeds become part of the soil and could sprout.

Don't compost weeds.

In the Garbage

The night before garbage pick-up is a good time to clean out the fridge. Put all the spoiled food into a bag, take it immediately to the can, and take the can to the curb. It is important to clean out the fridge regularly, and once a week is enough for most homes. If you do not, there will be rotting food stinking things up inside your refrigerator, and that can be very unhealthy.

Spoiled food left in the kitchen garbage for days could cause several things to happen. If you have pets, they might get into it, eat it, and become sick. Critters like mice, rats, ants, and other insects might get into it, and now that infestation needs dealt with. It might simply stink up the kitchen. The bacteria will multiply and could get on something else, especially if there is a hole in the bag.

When you throw it out in the garbage can outside, outdoor critters like mice, raccoons, rats, and even dogs or bears might find it and break in. (If the garbage containers are critter-proofed, that's not much of a concern.) If it's hot outside, the stink in the can might become truly awful. That doesn't make it wrong or make it OK to leave garbage pile up inside where it can be a health hazard. It's simply fair warning so you aren't surprised when it does happen.

Activity

Every week for a month, help clean out the spoiled food before the trash goes out. While you are doing that, check for food that needs to be eaten in the next week so it doesn't spoil, including frozen food that may be getting freezer burnt. Include those foods in the weekly meal plan (Chapter 12).

Quick Quiz

T/F   Spoiled food can become a safety hazard if not properly disposed of.

T/F   If the power is out for more than one hour, everything in the refrigerator and freezer has to be thrown out.

T/F   It is unsafe to eat food from a can that is bulging or leaking.

T/F   Bacteria and germs aren't a concern when preparing food.

T/F   If you can eat it, you can compost it.

Resources

Articles

*Composting
http://eartheasy.com/grow_compost.html

Composting at Home
http://www2.epa.gov/recycle/composting-home

Food Poisoning and Food Spoilage
http://culinaryarts.about.com/od/safetysanitation/a/bacteria.htm

How Composting Works
http://home.howstuffworks.com/composting.htm

*How Long does Food Stay Safe in a Power Outage?
http://www.foodsafety.gov/keep/charts/refridg_food.html

How to Tell When Food is Spoiled
http://www.mrbrown.com/blog/1998/08/how_to_tell_whe.html

How to Tell When Leftovers Go Bad
http://abcnews.go.com/Health/Germs/story?id=5560174&page=1&singlePage=true

*Safe Food Handling
http://www.fda.gov/Food/ResourcesForYou/Consumers/ucm255180.htm

Signs of Spoiled Canned Food
http://www.dummies.com/how-to/content/signs-of-spoiled-canned-food.html

Soldier Fly Larvae
http://extension.oregonstate.edu/gardening/big-maggots-your-compost-theyre-soldier-fly-larvae

CHAPTER THIRTEEN

*What to Compost
http://www.planetnatural.com/composting-101/what-to-use/

Books

Composting (Urban Gardening and Farming for Teens) by Brian Hanson-Harding

*Food Safety (New True Books: Health) by Christine Taylor-Butler

Food Safety: Staying Safe by Sally Lee

Let it Rot!: The Gardener's Guide to Composting (Third Edition) (Storey's Down-to-Earth Guides) by Stu Campbell

Worms Eat My Garbage: How to Set Up and Maintain a Worm Composting System, 2nd Edition by Mary Appelhof

Other

Compost Bin

Composter

Worm Composter

Videos

Composting for Kids
https://www.youtube.com/watch?v=TqfbxAi_9n8

*Doctor at Your Door: Spoiled Food, Expired Products Pose Kitchen Danger
http://abcnews.go.com/GMA/video/doctor-door-spoiled-food-expired-products-refrigerator-pose-13723418

FOOD SAFETY

How-to - Non-Electric Refrigerator - Prevent Food Spoilage - cheap
https://www.youtube.com/watch?v=YhUAO2Xm09g

How to Tell if Your Food Has Gone Bad
http://www.monkeysee.com/play/7754-how-to-tell-if-your-food-has-gone-bad

The Canning Diva's Quick Canning Tip- Identifying Spoiled Food
https://www.youtube.com/watch?v=H2uBdmg3NDs

*Scrubs - bacterial movement (My Cabbage episode)
https://www.youtube.com/watch?v=VK2vpOh5wws

Spoiled Meat
https://www.youtube.com/watch?v=PAmUZZa87GI

Fruit and Vegetables Decomposition, Time-lapse
https://www.youtube.com/watch?v=c0En-_BVbGc

Worm Composting 101
https://www.youtube.com/watch?v=6UYac_8rWec

{Fourteen}

Follow a Recipe

It may seem obvious to anyone who has been cooking for long, but everyone should be able to follow a recipe. Following a recipe sounds simple, but it is a skill to learn like any other. Even basic facts like "T" means "tablespoon" while "t" means "teaspoon" are details everyone needs to learn when they start cooking.

Basic Tools

Some things are easy to understand, such as measuring cups, but others need a little practice. Several of these may be unusual in a modern kitchen, but they are good to have in an emergency because they don't need electricity. Recipes generally assume you know the correct tools to use, unless they are in a "My First" cookbook. (My personal favorite, and most-used, cookbook is a "My First" cookbook.)

Egg Beater

Egg beaters are like a small, hand-powered mixer. They can't handle thick dough (like cookies), but if you need to "beat egg whites to a peak," you'll get there much faster with this than with a whisk.

Electric Mixer

An electric, or stand, mixer is one of the most basic kitchen tools in most homes. They have a lot of uses and when most recipes tell you to "mix," they assume you will use an electric mixer. They range from simple older models to complex newer "food processors" that can mix bread, chop food, and so much more.

Personally, I find a mixer bulky to use, store, and move around, and more work to clean. In my life, I have found two recipes (frosting and marshmallows) that I truly cannot make without an electric mixer. Instead, I use a pastry blender or whisk for almost everything. A few things I even quite mix by (thoroughly cleaned) hand.

Food Processor

Mini food processors are a fast way to chop and blend food. We use a small one that is perfect for small batches. I use ours for salsa, which maxes out how much it can hold.

Many stand mixers are also food processors and can, obviously, handle much larger amounts.

Pastry Blender

I use my pastry blender instead of an electric mixer to mix thicker consistency dough such as cookies. If the final step of a recipe is to form it into a ball, it's probably a good candidate for a pastry blender.

CHAPTER FOURTEEN

Slow Cooker

"Crock Pot" is actually a trademarked name, although it's often used to refer to any slow cooker. With a slow cooker, you put the food in and let it cook for eight or more hours. That means you can start it in the morning, spend all day at school or at work while it cooks, and it will be ready to eat at dinner time with no (or little) effort when you return home. You can also start a meal before going to bed and have it ready for breakfast.

Slow cookers are a great way to prepare meals ahead of time and are amazing. You can even bake bread and desserts in them. No joke!

The off-grid version is called a "Wonderbag."

Whisk

A whisk can be used instead of an electric mixer for thinner consistency foods. If the final step of the recipe is to "pour" the batter, it's probably a good candidate for whisking. The best basic technique to swish the whisk from side to side until everything is thoroughly mixed, as shown in a Video in the Resources section.

There are actually a surprising variety of sizes and styles, but a basic teardrop shaped whisk works for most home cooking needs. In our house, we have a small rubber-coated one we use to mix scrambled eggs in the pan, a larger metal one (my favorite for most uses), and a tiny one used to mix small amounts of ingredients.

Rubberized or silicone coatings are nice for pans with anti-stick coatings that a metal whisk can scratch. The coating can be damaged over time so they may not last as long as metal whisks.

Basic Techniques

Browning, searing, roasting, frying, chopping, dicing.... The list of techniques used in cooking is seemingly endless, and not entirely in English. A fair number of them, like browning and frying, are self-explanatory, but some are a bit tougher to understand.

Chop

It's not hard to figure out that this means to cut something up. What is less obvious is that it means to cut it into pieces that are bite-size, or possibly even smaller.

Dice

Food that has been diced is cut into pieces that are smaller than bite size. Generally, that is somewhere around the size of a pea. If you think about the smallest piece you can cut that food item into without having it fall apart or be too small to spear with a fork, you are probably in the right ballpark.

Mince

Mincing is generally not done by hand, or at least not without a specialized gadget. When food is minced, it is cut into pieces small enough that you can't easily pick up one part with a utensil. Mincing is most commonly reserved for herbs, such as garlic.

Sauté

This is a form of stovetop cooking that uses a small amount of oil (most often olive oil or butter) over fairly high heat. Food is cut into small pieces so it cooks quickly.

Preheat the pan and make sure to stir or toss the food constantly so it doesn't burn. Sautéing usually only takes a few minutes (less than 10) and is rarely the only technique used in preparing a meal.

Although both frying and sautéing use oil to cook food, they are very different techniques. In frying, food is entirely submerged in oil while it is cooked. In sautéing, only a small amount of oil is used. A different cooking technique is normally used to finish preparing the meal.

Using Measuring Tools

It isn't complicated, but it's important to make sure that if a recipe calls for one cup or one teaspoon (etc.), you use exactly that amount. If an ingredient is heaped up over the top or doesn't reach the top, you don't have exactly the needed amount and your recipe may not come out right. You can use the straight side of a knife to smooth the top of measuring spoons or cups.

There are the most common abbreviations used for amounts in cooking.

T or tbsp. = tablespoon

t or tsp. = teaspoon

c. = cup

oz. = ounce

lb. = pound

Brown sugar is the only common ingredient that needs to be packed when you measure it. Recipes always assume brown sugar is packed unless otherwise specified.

Activity

Find a recipe for something you like. Make and eat it.

Quick Quiz

T/F   Thorough hand-washing is the first step in food prep.

T/F   Sautéing and frying are exactly the same thing.

T/F   Measuring accurately is important, particularly in baking.

T/F   Making a meal without electric appliances and gadgets is impossible.

T/F   An egg beater and a mixer are similar.

Resources

Use your discretion when choosing to teach anyone how to use sharp, hot, or otherwise potentially dangerous items.

Articles

How to Sauté

http://www.wikihow.com/Saut%C3%A9

CHAPTER FOURTEEN

Recipes and Cooking
http://kidshealth.org/kid/recipes/

Books

ChopChop: The Kids' Guide to Cooking Real Food with Your Family by Sally Sampson

Cooking with Children: 15 Lessons for Children, Age 7 and Up, Who Really Want to Learn to Cook by Marion Cunningham

Knife Skills by Marcus Wareing

Learn to Cook 101 -- Step-by-Step Cooking Lessons for All Ages by the Cooking Dude, John Choisser

Teens Cook: How to Cook What You Want to Eat by Jill and Megan Carle

Other

Oxo Good Grips Egg Beater

Hamilton Beach 6 Speed Classic Stand Mixer

Black and Decker One Touch Electric Chopper

Winco 5 Blade Pastry Blender, Stainless Steel

Programmable Crock-Pot Cook and Carry Slow-Cooker

Scouting-Specific

New Cuisines Badge
http://forgirls.girlscouts.org/home/badgeexplorer/#new-cuisines

Simple Meals Badge
http://forgirls.girlscouts.org/home/badgeexplorer/#simple-meals

Videos

How to Chop Vegetables
https://www.youtube.com/watch?v=7iP_X0ztjJQ

How to Measure Wet and Dry Ingredients - Kitchen Conundrums
with Thomas Joseph
https://www.youtube.com/watch?v=qzr82EuiJu0

How to Sauté Chicken with Julia Child
https://www.youtube.com/watch?v=ZqOzcndykQM

Cooking Tips: How to Use a Pastry Blender
https://www.youtube.com/watch?v=T4gObuCCFvE

Science: the Best Way to Use a Whisk
https://www.youtube.com/watch?v=zglSRFlFH-s

Knife Skills (Dice, Mince, Chop, Slice)
https://www.youtube.com/watch?v=AVQkqKUSZ2M

{Fifteen}

Hygiene and Sanitation

Basic hygiene is primarily about keeping your body clean and free of germs. Sanitation is about disposing of sewage and solid waste in a hygienic manner, so they don't spread diseases.

Basic Hygiene

This includes all the activities parents and grandparents harp about:

- Brush your teeth every morning, before bedtime (every day), and possibly after lunch.
- Floss your teeth at least once a day.
- Shower and wash your hair regularly. In hot weather and when you exercise, this normally means once a day. In cold weather, it could be every two or three days, depending on your activity level and how stinky you get.
- Wear deodorant. Every day.
- If your hair is longer than an inch or two inches, comb

or brush it at least once a day. Even if you don't plan on going anywhere.

- Put on clean underwear and socks every single day, normally after you take a shower. If it's a day you don't take a shower, change them when you would take a shower just so you don't forget and wear them for more than a day.

- After a shower, everything you put on should be clean, and you should use deodorant every day.

- Wash your hands for 20 seconds every time you use the toilet and before you eat. Wash the top, the palms, and in between your fingers with soap. Running water over them of rubbing a bit of soap around on your palms (and nothing else) doesn't result in germ-free hands.

- Keep your nails cut short. When there is dirt under them, use a nail brush to clean it out, then wash your hands. (See previous bullet point.)

- In a pinch, hand sanitizer can be used to sanitize other items, but be sure not to eat any of it.

Survival Sanitation

Sanitation focuses on disposing of waste in a way that promotes health and well-being. A cat covering what it leaves in the litter box is possibly the most rudimentary form of sanitation because it helps keep them from stepping in the waste and either tracking it around or ingesting it when they clean their fur.

Clearly, people don't lick themselves or their shoes clean, but the same concepts apply. In our normal, modern lives, sanitation is almost entirely taken for granted. Our waste products simply disappear down a pipe or into a septic tank, hauled away to places we never see. (Septic tanks have to be emptied into septic trunks every few years.)

In an emergency, these systems stop working. If there is no power to run the sewage treatment plant or to pump water from the well to the house and then out to the septic field, waste will simply back up in the pipes until it finally explodes out the end of the pipes and into your home. Definitely not sanitary.

Basic Cleaning

Alcohol (the main ingredient in most store-bought hand sanitizers) kills many germs and bacteria. So does soap. Use them, especially on your hands and face, but also on objects. Alcohol can be a quick way to sanitize things like thermometers and cups.

In a true survival situation, properly washing or not properly washing your hands after using the toilet could quite literally be the difference between life and death. Many diseases are transmitted through fecal matter (poop) and not washing your hands could leave trace amounts on your hands. Later, if you wipe your mouth or your eyes or your nose, guess what just entered your body? That's right—whatever was left on your hands after you didn't wash properly. In regular life, unwashed hands after using the toilet regularly lands people in the emergency room.

HYGIENE AND SANITATION

Dish Washing

In normal life, dishes may be rinsed, put in the dishwasher, washed, left to dry, and then put away. In an emergency, the first step of cleaning may be to take a handful of dirt or sand and use it to scrub stuck-on food off of pots and pans.

In the woods or a true emergency situation, the real first step is to eat everything on the plate, then put some water on the plate to rinse off any residue and pour it into the cup. Swish dirty utensils in that to clean them off, and then drink the water. Yes, you read it correctly—drink the dirty water to get every last morsel of nutrition and to minimize any food waste that might draw critters. The only "dirt" in it is bits of the same food you just ate.

Three dishpans are required for the actual dishwashing. Fill the first dishpan with hot water and biodegradable soap. Wash the plates, cups, and utensils. The second tub has hot rinse water. The third has water (any temperature) with sterilizing tablets added. After soaking dishes in the last tub for one minute, fully submerged, lay them out to dry. Dishes can be dried with a towel, but that is more likely to accidentally put germs on them than simply air-drying them.

For pots and pans, pour a small amount of the water inside each one instead of submerging them into the dishpan. The outside doesn't need cleaned, after all! As you finish with the water, pour it through a tea towel or other piece of fabric to strain out debris. The debris goes into your trash. The waste water is dumped away from the campsite and at least 75 steps from any body of water.

Do not handle clean dishes with dirty hands or the once-clean dishes will be contaminated and need rewashed.

Food Waste

In a survival situation, disposing of toilet waste and food waste are both extremely important. Toilet waste should be obvious, but food waste may not be as obvious if you don't eat much fresh food. Food rots. Bacteria grow in rotting food and animals, including rats, are drawn to any food source. Bacteria cause disease. Animals leave droppings and more, different bacteria.

In a long-term survival situation, there will initially be fairly large amounts of once-refrigerated and frozen food that begins to rot and form a biohazard. After that disappears, food waste will be less of a problem because there will be less food and so less will be wasted/thrown away. Hunger is a much bigger problem in true emergencies than food waste.

Toilet Waste

Toilet waste, on the other hand, will be an issue as long as people are living. If there are large numbers of people around, this will almost certainly contaminate the water supply and it will need treated to be drinkable (Chapter 8.)

If a small number of people have become lost, had an accident, or are otherwise in more of a wilderness-survival situation where they are looking for aid, this is less of a concern *as long as they are on the move.*

The solution here really goes back to the cat and its litter box: dig a hole no more than 6 inches deep, deposit your waste, cover it, and move on. If you will be staying in one place for up to three days or so, dig the trench 1 - 3 feet deep and put a layer of dirt over the contents after each use. It gradually fills in and the smell isn't a problem. For humans, this is called a slit trench, cat hole, or straddle trench.

If you are in a short-term emergency in a building with no running water, you can't simply continue to use the toilet as normal because there is no water to wash away the waste. It will fill up the toilet and overflow unless you pour water over it to "flush."

You can also put a garbage bag in the toilet, between the seat and the bowl, to capture all the waste. Tie off the bag between uses to cut down on odor and to keep insects from landing on the waste and then on your food. Adding saw dust, coal ash, or cat litter should help reduce the smell.

A five gallon bucket with a toilet seat on it is another option. Two more are camping and composting toilets, but those must be purchased in advance. If you live somewhere prone to natural emergencies such as tornados, hurricanes, or earthquakes, buying one of these to keep on hand is a good idea.

Activity

For one day, make a list of all the waste products you dispose of. Which ones might create an unsanitary condition if they were just left sitting around? How long do you think that would take? How was it taken care of in your regular life? How might it be taken care of in an emergency?

Quick Quiz

T/F   Survival sanitation methods vary based on how many people must be cared for.

T/F   Toilet waste and food waste are two primary concerns with survival sanitation.

T/F   Basic hygiene includes washing your hands, brushing your teeth, and generally staying clean.

T/F   In a long-term survival situation, food waste becomes a larger concern than toilet waste.

T/F   Proper survival sanitation technique helps keep nearby water sources potable longer.

Resources

Articles

*Camp-Washing Dishes
http://scoutmastercg.com/how-to-wash-dishes-when-camping/

*Emergency Sanitation
http://www.practicalsurvivor.com/emergencysanitation

Homemade Deodorant
http://thesurvivalmom.com/breast-lump-led-homemade-deodorant/

REI on Sanitation
http://www.rei.com/learn/expert-advice/hygiene-sanitation.html

HYGIENE AND SANITATION

Straddle Trench
http://www.survivalworld.com/hygiene-sanitation/straddle-trench.html#.VRLZquFIOSo

*Urban Survival Sanitation
http://offgridsurvival.com/urbansurvivalsanitation/

Books

Compost Toilets: A Practical DIY Guide by Dave Darby

Other

Luggable Loo Portable 5 Gallon Toilet

Campsuds (biodegradable soap)

Nature's Head Composting Toilet

Emergency Toilet Seat Lid (fits 5 gallon buckets)

US Military E-Tool

Steramine Sterilizing Tablets

Scouting-Specific

Leave No Trace
http://www.scouting.org/scoutsource/OutdoorProgram/LeaveNoTrace.aspx

Public Health Merit Badge
http://meritbadge.org/wiki/index.php/Public_Health

Videos

Bushcraft Camp Hygiene Series Part 4- Improvised Hand Sanitation
https://www.youtube.com/watch?v=C_kera_ckCM

Survival Sanitation with Dr. Bones
https://www.youtube.com/watch?v=GnxVkGhfpEs

{Sixteen}

Cleaning

An important part of both hygiene and sanitation is cleaning. In addition to a clean body, washing dishes, doing laundry, and generally keeping your environment clean are all important.

In an emergency, many of the common store-bought cleaners we use may not be available. It doesn't even have to be a the-end-of-the-world-as-we-know-it (TEOTWAWKI) emergency. It could be as simple as someone having a nasty virus and throwing up all over the floor and not having enough cleaning products when the stores, or roads, are closed.

Most of the cleaning we need to do is quite simple: when you make a mess, clean it up immediately. The longer it sets, the harder it is to clean. If the problem is something sticky or hard to remove (like eggs baked onto a pan), soak it for a few hours or overnight and then clean it.

Another big chunk of cleaning is simply wiping up messes as they accumulate. The steps in our house need swept regularly because cat hair accumulates on them. Lights and ceilings need cobwebs removed, and most horizontal surfaces need dusted.

Once you get beyond those basic maintenance activities, houses need some deeper cleaning done a few times a year. There are a few multipurpose products that can clean almost anything. Baking soda, castile soap, and vinegar are three of the most versatile of these. (Castile soap is a biodegradable soap made entirely of plant oils; it contains no animal products.)

The shortest possible introduction to each of these three cleaners is below. Entire books have been written about all their uses. Take some time to go out and learn a bit more about how many things they can do. They really are amazing.

> **Note:** Baking soda mixes very well with vinegar and with castile soap, but *do not* mix castile soap and vinegar. Because of their chemical properties, they essentially cancel each other out and end up doing nothing useful.

Baking Soda

First and foremost, baking soda gets rid of funky smells pretty much anywhere. Fridge, sneakers, garbage can, bathroom, armpits, musty carpets–it's all the same to baking soda. Sprinkle a bit or leave a container open to absorb smells almost anywhere. (Except your armpits; that requires a pastier consistency.)

As a powder, it absorbs oils and grease, making clean-up easier. It also does an impressive job of cleaning a wide variety of surfaces, including countertops and bathrooms.

As a paste, it can clean stained plastic lunch box containers and remove the dirt and wax from fruits and vegetables. Of course, it can also be used in deodorant and toothpaste.

Castile Soap

Dr. Bronner's is by far the most common and popular brand. The short version of what to use Castile soap for: if a liquid soap can clean it, odds are good Castile soap can too.

A slightly more detailed list includes shampoo, shower soap, bathroom cleaner, laundry detergent, dishwasher detergent, toothpaste, veggie wash, toilet cleaner, baby wash, shaving cream.... The list of uses for castile soap goes on and on and on.

Laundry

Laundry is generally a simple process: sort, wash, dry, fold, put away. Under normal circumstances, washing and drying is done in an electric washer at home or at a laundromat. In an emergency, the washing part may need to be done using an off-grid gadget and drying may be done outside on a clothesline. Sorting, folding, and putting things away is the same with or without power.

Sorting

Sorting has three main components: color, temperature, and wash cycle. These depend, in part, on dirtiness, and sturdiness. The main divisions for color are white, red, and everything else. Reds are particularly likely to "bleed." This means that the color leaves that fabric and goes into another next to it, permanently dying all or part of it pink. Closely related colors such as pinks and oranges can go in with reds because it's hard to see any change from a little extra red dye with those.

Whites are washed separately from colors since there is no dye in them at all to fade onto anything else. They may also need something extra added to keep the whites sparkling, such as bleach, OxiClean™, or a cup of baking soda. When there are really large piles of laundry, they can be sorted further so that greens, browns, light blues, dark blues, jeans, etc. are separate loads.

Fabrics that are either germy (socks and underwear) or that need to not be germy when you are finished (anything that touches food, such as dish towels or placemats) should be washed in hot water.

Bathroom towels are also often washed in hot water because they tend to be damp most of the time, so they can get musty. Towels and sheets are normally separate loads from clothing because they take enough space to be an entire load, all by themselves, and towels take longer to dry.

Most other items can be washed in cold. Anything that has a stain that needs removed should *not* go in hot water because that "sets" the stain, making it extremely hard to remove. The stain needs treated before it is washed, aka "pretreated."

CHAPTER SIXTEEN

Washing

Soap nuts and homemade laundry detergent are both effective. (Part of the point of this book is being able survive and make due without things we normally take for granted.) Put one of those or your regular detergent in with the clothing and follow the directions on your machine.

If you decide to make your own laundry detergent, be sure to check if your washer is HE (High Efficiency) or not. HE washers use different detergent than older models. The HE detergent doesn't make as many suds. Using regular detergent in an HE washer can lead to a HUGE mess. Just don't do it.

Off-Grid

There are a variety of off-grid washing machines available, but they really fall into two major styles. One resembles an old-fashioned washboard. The wet laundry has soap added and then is rubbed over ridged plastic or metal to work out any dirt and stains. Then it is rinsed and hung up to dry. Zote is a popular Mexican soap that works particularly well for this.

The second method is closer to a modern spin-wash cycle. The items are put in a closed container with an agitator, soap, and water. A person manually turns the wash tub or powers the agitator to work the soapy water through the garment. The water is poured out and fresh water is put in to rinse the soapy water out of the garment before it is hung up to dry.

Drying

Put all the damp clothing into the dryer with whatever fabric softener or anti-static remedy your family uses. Make sure the lint screen is empty and run the machine. When it finishes, confirm that everything is dry and either remove it from the machine or finish drying it. Empty the lint screen. (Lint build up can lead to fires, so checking twice is not a bad thing.)

Dryer balls are an effective and cost-efficient way to battle static and soften clothing. Adding vinegar and water to the fabric softener reservoir for the dryer is an effective alternative fabric softener.

Off-Grid

Hang items on a clothesline or drying rack to dry. If it will be raining, bring them in before the rain starts and either hang them up inside to finish drying or take them back outside when the shower ends, if it's short.

Sorting and Putting Away

Separate items by who wears them, where they are stored (dresser drawers or closet), and what they are (socks, long sleeve shirts, short sleeve shirts, etc.). Then put them away. If anything needs ironed, put it where ironing goes.

Vinegar

Window cleaning. Wood floors and cutting boards. Killing weeds.

Removing wallpaper. Cleaning stainless steel. Vinegar practically works miracles. For most purposes, vinegar is mixed with water.

Be very careful of using vinegar in a toilet. It can eat away at the wax ring used to secure the toilet, especially if it's used regularly.

Activity

Use baking soda, castile soap, or vinegar to clean something.

Quick Quiz

T/F   Baking soda removes odors.

T/F   Vinegar is good for cleaning wood.

T/F   Baking soda and vinegar can be used together.

T/F   Soap nuts are an all-natural laundry detergent.

T/F   It is impossible to wash laundry without electricity.

Resources

Articles

10 Uses for Baking Soda: Cleaning Your Bathroom
http://home.howstuffworks.com/home-improvement/household-hints-tips/cleaning-organizing/uses-for-baking-soda-cleaning-your-bathroom-ga.htm

10 Ways to Clean with Vinegar
http://www.huffingtonpost.com/2013/03/24/vinegar-cleaning-recipes_n_2933347.html

12 Great Ways to Use Castile Soap
http://www.care2.com/greenliving/12-great-ways-to-use-castile-soap.html

CLEANING

21 Cleaning Problems You Can Solve with Baking Soda
http://www.goodhousekeeping.com/home/cleaning/tips/a25577/baking-soda-cleaning-uses/

Cleaning with Vinegar
http://versatilevinegar.org/usesandtips.html

Don't Mix Vinegar and Castile Soap
http://www.liverenewed.com/2012/10/days-green-clean-common-green-cleaning-mistake.html

How to Care for Every Fabric in Your Wardrobe (Tween, Teen)
http://www.dailymail.co.uk/femail/article-3043211/How-care-fabric-wardrobe-revealed.html

Kitchen Safety: How to Put Out a Grease Fire (Tween, Teen)
http://www.thekitchn.com/kitchen-safety-how-to-put-out-138233

The Many Uses of Castile Soap
http://www.liverenewed.com/2011/04/the-many-uses-of-castile-soap.html

The Survival Mom's Mini-Guide to Switching from Store-Bought to Homemade
http://thesurvivalmom.com/wp-content/uploads/2015/02/HomemadeEGuide.pdf

Books

Baking Soda Secrets: Discover the Many Miraculous Baking Soda Homemade Solutions You Never Knew About by Angie S

Baking Soda: DIY Cleaning Hacks, Discover the Cleaning, Health and Hygiene Hacks of Baking Soda by Liza Leake

Green Cleaning 101: DIY Natural Cleaning Solutions with Vinegar and Other Frugal Resources That You Already Have by Sustainable Stevie

The Organically Clean Home: 150 Everyday Organic Cleaning Products You Can Make Yourself--The Natural, Chemical-Free Way by Becky Rapinchuk

Vinegar: Over 400 Various, Versatile, and Very Good Uses You've Probably Never Thought Of by Vicki Lansky

Other

Castile Soap (Dr. Bronner's)

Wool Dryer Balls

Scrubba

SoapNuts

Japanese Laundry Wash Basin

Wonderwash

Videos

10 Awesome Vinegar Life Hacks You Should Know
https://www.youtube.com/watch?v=RCgIdfuQAD4

Baking Soda is Awesome for Cleaning! 10 Cleaning Uses for Baking Soda (Clean My Space)
https://www.youtube.com/watch?v=4ciahsfuzXM

Non-toxic Kitchen Cleaning with Baking Soda (Pots and Pans)
https://www.youtube.com/watch?v=OH2s9QWbPpM

White Vinegar Cleaning and Laundry Uses
https://www.youtube.com/watch?v=XDiPx16dtjc

{Part 4}
Health and First Aid

If we don't have our health, we don't have anything. Most of us have heard that saying at some point. I'm not sure to whom it is currently attributed, but some Neanderthal mom probably told a variation of it to her family and so it has come to is, down through the ages.

The first and most basic aspects of exercise and good diet have already been covered. Being healthy involves more than that, though. It involves not being sick. All of these topics play into either avoiding getting sick or recovering more quickly, or both.

In daily life, it sometimes seems easy to rely on medical care and doctor visits fixing anything that goes wrong, but that's not a good approach. Taking care of our bodies and knowing how to fix smaller problems is a much better choice.

Family Medical Issues: Knowing the critical allergy and medical needs of those around you, especially family, and how to help them in an emergency is an often-overlooked aspect of health and first aid that could save lives.

Knowing the medical allergies of your parents and siblings could help *a lot* in an emergency situation. Everyone in the family should know about any serious allergies, regular medications, or serious illnesses the others have. In an emergency, it could be the difference between life and death.

First Aid Classes: Even very young children can learn how to bandage a cut. That is the first step in first aid. Once you are comfortable with that, move on to something harder, like removing a splinter or making a sling. If you keep building your skills, you should eventually find yourself becoming very good at helping others when they are injured.

As a teen, you can take Wilderness First Aid and possibly EMT training to enable you to handle more complicated medical situations. Being an EMT is an actual paid job, and one that is highly portable. (That means you can find a job in a lot of places as you move around in life unlike, say, surf instructor or ski patrol, which are not highly portable jobs.)

Home Remedies: For almost all of human history, home remedies have been the most common form of medical treatment. While modern medicine spent decades looking down on these remedies as worthless, studies have know shown many of them to be very helpful. This is a huge area and only a very few remedies are discussed.

A lot of these are food-based. Chicken soup for a cold. Lemon tea and honey for a sore throat. Chamomile tea to calm. Warm milk to induce sleep. These are often very easy to make and use, and very difficult (possibly impossible) to overdose on or misuse. Can you image overdosing on warm milk or chicken soup?

Calling 911: Discussing how and when to call 911 seems silly and like an obvious waste of ink. The truth is that the number for Emergency Services isn't always 911, and not every situation that requires emergency responders (police, ambulance) requires a 911 call.

In a true emergency, knowing what information is needed and to whom it must go is the definition of a life-and-death situation. Having non-emergency calls go to a different dispatcher than the emergency calls can save lives, especially in an emergency. Even in a non-emergency, many areas have 911 systems that are over-burdened by non-emergency calls, just as emergency rooms can be overburdened by people with the flu and other illnesses that don't truly need the resources of an emergency room.

{Seventeen}

Family Medical Issues

Almost every family has some medical issues, even simple problems like seasonal allergies. By the time you are in elementary school you should be able memorize any truly critical health problems, like life-threatening allergies. If a family member has diabetes, takes medication regularly, or has severe allergies, emergency services providers having that information could be a life or death issue.

No one expects you to remember that Grandma take Plavix and Lipitor, has a mild allergy to penicillin, and has blocked arteries. If you can remember that she has a pillbox in her purse or on the window sill near the sink, or maybe even where she keeps her pill bottles, that is enough for emergency service responders to check her meds in an emergency. Even remembering "there is something wrong in her head" will help them.

It is important that you memorize any truly severe allergies in your immediate family. If your mom questions the server every single time to make sure there is not chance walnuts have touched anything near

172

her food, it's fairly easy to remember that walnut allergy, if for no other reason than it starts to get annoying to hear. Be sure to tell doctors/EMTs/etc. about the allergies if no other adults are around.

Medical History

As you grow older, you can do more. Learning any medical allergies is a good next step. What allergies do family members have? How severe are they? What reaction to they have? Getting hives is very different from going into anaphylactic shock. If anyone has an EpiPen®, it is very important for everyone in the family to know where to find it (even tiny kids can direct others to it) and for anyone who is old enough and responsible enough to know how to administer it.

Creating a medical/health history of your close family members and knowing what your immediate family, up to grandparents, died of is important, too. Doctors always ask new patients for this, so it will help you for the rest of your life. If there is a history of heart disease, diabetes, stroke, cancer, tumors, or anything else significant in either the personal or family history for anyone in your family, telling that to a medical care provider could be critical. If three out of four grandparents died of strokes or heart attacks, that could be good information for the medics to have to help in a faster diagnosis.

That doesn't mean you have to memorize the entire health history. There are apps for that. Even if you don't have the app, if someone in the family has it (with all the information in it) and you know where to find it, that is more than good enough.

Medical Equipment and Essential Medicines

As mentioned above, knowing how to find and administer an EpiPen could be the difference between life and death for a family member, but that isn't the only key medicine/medical equipment you should know.

Does anyone use an oxygen tank? Usually only elderly or very sick people need them, but knowing how to help them hook up a new tank could make a huge difference for them.

How about insulin? Does anyone need insulin shots or use a pump? Do you know where to find their supplies and how to help them if they need it? Do you know what to give them if their blood sugar goes too low, or how to tell that is happening? Do they carry something with them for blood sugar dips and spikes?

Is there anyone with a serious heart problem? Do they have nitroglycerin (nitro) tablets or spray if they run into problems? Can you find them? Do you know how to administer them? The tablets typically go under the tongue or between the gums and cheek where they dissolve quickly into the bloodstream.

Assist Other People

How can you help others in an emergency?

- Perform first aid.
- Write notes to give emergency providers.
- Write notes dictated by emergency provider.

- Help people find their loved ones.
- Reach things in small, high, low, or otherwise hard-to-reach spaces.
- Actually pick someone up and carry them to safety. (Most people aren't able to do this, even full-grown adults.)
- Stay calm, or at least stay still. Panic can kill.

Activity

Have a family meeting and review any serious health problems each of you has. Then go over any problems close family members have, including grandparents and aunts and uncles. Make sure everyone knows where to find and how to administer critical medicine. Finally, determine a location everyone can access where you can keep all your important medical information, or download an app and fill in all the information for your family, with their help.

Quick Quiz

T/F   It is not important to know about serious allergies and health problems for close family members.

T/F   Knowing how to administer an EpiPen if anyone in your family has one is a good idea.

T/F   Panicking in an emergency is never a problem.

T/F   Diabetes can be a serious medical condition that requires immediate care.

CHAPTER SEVENTEEN

T/F   Writing notes is one way to help others in an emergency.

Resources

Articles

*Gathering Family Medical Information
http://www.mayoclinic.org/healthy-living/adult-health/in-depth/medical-history/art-20044961

My Family Health Portrait (Family Project)
https://familyhistory.hhs.gov/FHH/html/index.html

Surgeon General's Family Health History Initiative
http://www.hhs.gov/familyhistory/index.html

Why is it Important to Know My Family Medical History?
http://ghr.nlm.nih.gov/handbook/inheritance/familyhistory

Books

Your Family Health Organizer: Record Parents' and Kids' Medical Information All in One Place by Jodie Pappas (Family Project)

Other

*Family Medical Info (app)

Ahh Ha Medical Records Organizer Kit [Professionally Printed Tabs for USE in a Three Ring Binder] (family project)

{Eighteen}

First Aid Classes

These skills are listed from very basic skills even a very young child can learn up to to advanced skills that taught at community colleges or through volunteering as an EMT with a local fire station.

Most of these require training and recertification every few years. Recertification means retaking the class and repassing the test at the end of it. Please do not attempt anything beyond basic first aid without training.

Basic First Aid

First Aid starts out with simple tasks like basic wound care, removing a splinter, and treating a fever.

Basic wound care involves cleaning/washing, disinfecting, and finally bandaging the wound.

A splinter is most commonly removed with a pair of tweezers.

Over the counter medicines, cold compresses (a cold damp cloth) on the forehead, and cool baths are the most common remedies for a fever.

CPR (Cardio Pulmonary Respiration)

CPR is used when someone isn't breathing. Generally, this is because their heart isn't beating and their blood isn't flowing. It involves chest compressions (pushing down on the person's chest) and rescue breathing. Chest compressions are the more important of the two, to the point that rescue breathing sometimes isn't even taught. Once you start CPR, you must continue until help arrives, someone else takes over, or you are no longer physically able to continue.

CPR won't restart a heart, but it does keep some blood flowing to prevent or reduce brain damage.

Basic CPR is a four hour class, although it is now also available online or partially online. It is also possible to take Infant & Child CPR, which is approximately another two hours, but that is much more difficult to find. The Red Cross has long been one of the premiere providers of CPR certification and their courses are easy to find, anywhere in the country.

Wilderness First Aid (WFA)

Wilderness First Aid is a two to two and a half day class that teaches skills for responding to emergencies in areas emergency responders can't get to quickly. WFA is for people 14 years or older, although it may be difficult to find a class if you are under 18. There is often a chance to take CPR immediately before or along with WFA because if you are in the back country, you really want to have that skill as well.

Because of the name, being in the distant woods or on top of a mountain either hiking or camping are what come to mind first when you think of Wilderness First Aid, but it is useful in urban disaster situations such as the aftermath of tornadoes, earthquakes, and hurricanes, as well as more mundane situations such as someone becoming injured on a day hike a mile or two from the end of the trail.

It's amazing how long it can take Emergency Medial Services (EMS) to reach someone over a mile up a trail. Having someone in the group who can assess them and help get everyone moving toward safety is a huge help if that happens.

EMTs and Paramedics

Emergency Medical Technicians (EMTs) and paramedics are part of ambulance crews who work to stabilize people for transport to a hospital or triage center in an emergency. They have had quite a bit of training–at least three full weeks for EMTs–and are typically required to be at least 18 years old. When you call 911 for a medical emergency or accident, they are the medical person who examines you.

As you would guess, their skills include handling a wide variety of traumas as well as more common medical situations such as broken bones, trauma, and childbirth. EMTs assess patients to determine if they need to go to the hospital emergency room, see their own doctor, keep an eye on things at home, or are fine.

Activity

The next time someone has a minor injury, help treat it.

Quick Quiz

T/F   Elementary kids can take Wilderness First Aid.

T/F   CPR is a two day, 20 hour class.

T/F   Wilderness First Aid can be helpful even in urban areas.

T/F   When you bandage a cut, that is Basic First Aid.

T/F   Every First Aid class is good for a certain number of years, then you need to recertify.

Resources

Articles

*Illnesses and Injuries
http://kidshealth.org/kid/ill_injure/

Performing CPR
http://firstaid.about.com/od/cpr/ht/06_cpr.htm

Red Cross Classes
http://www.redcross.org/take-a-class

Wilderness First Aid Training
http://www.nols.edu/wmi/courses/wildfirstaid.shtml

FIRST AID CLASSES

Books

American Red Cross First Aid/CPR/AED Participant's Manual by the American Red Cross

The American Red Cross First Aid and Safety Handbook by the American Red Cross

Wilderness First Responder: How To Recognize, Treat, And Prevent Emergencies In The Backcountry by Buck Tilton

Other

Medibag First Aid Kit

*Key Chain CPR Mask

Scouting-Specific (increasing levels of difficulty)

First Aid Badge
http://forgirls.girlscouts.org/home/badgeexplorer/#brownie-first-aid

First Aid Badge
http://forgirls.girlscouts.org/home/badgeexplorer/#junior-first-aid

First Aid Badge
http://forgirls.girlscouts.org/home/badgeexplorer/#cadette-first-aid

First Aid Badge
http://forgirls.girlscouts.org/home/badgeexplorer/#senior-first-aid

First Aid Badge
http://forgirls.girlscouts.org/home/badgeexplorer/#11th-12th Graders-first-aid

First Aid Merit Badge
http://meritbadge.org/wiki/index.php/First_Aid

CHAPTER EIGHTEEN

Videos

Advice on Keeping Children Cool During Hot Weather
https://www.youtube.com/watch?v=36KrCuJ6uoE

First Aid - Dealing with Choking (British Red Cross)
https://www.youtube.com/watch?v=Wuo893OC0yE&list=PLjXQQ4--O4ljxbXgZetcpmXOoc6-oElFW

Learn Hands-Only CPR from the American Red Cross
https://www.youtube.com/watch?v=-Yqk5cHXsko

Patient Assessment Demonstration - Wilderness First Aid
https://www.youtube.com/watch?v=OhFy4FwT5DA

{Nineteen}

Home Remedies

For most sicknesses and or injuries, there are lots of treatment choices. Some are effective, some aren't. Some are home remedies. Others are over-the-counter or doctor-prescribed medicine. Different things work for different people.

Home remedies are common for some problems, like the hiccups. It takes severe, long-term hiccups to go beyond home care standards such as a spoonful of sugar and getting scared. Colds (chicken soup) and fever (cold compresses and baths) have long had home remedies, as well as the medicines commonly used now.

The more serious the condition, the more likely it is that professional medical intervention is needed. Home remedies are best used for minor injuries or to buy time until professional help can be reached, for more serious injuries and illnesses.

Some home remedies are herbal medicine, a huge, complex field in and of itself. This section includes a variety of simple, popular, and multi-use remedies. You may know some, but many will probably be new to you. Only a few of the most common of the dozens of uses are included for each home remedy.

In a related field, essential oils (EOs) have become very popular again. Essential oils are also derived from plants. The only one discussed here is tea tree oil, but there are essential oils for nearly any illness, injury, or physical malady imaginable.

EOs are highly concentrated and some are dangerous, even deadly, if taken internally. They should be added to a carrier lotion or oil (sold by the companies that sell EOs) and used externally–on your skin.

For many ailments, the best treatment is a combination of oils. Companies that specialize in essential oils such as Eden's Garden, dōTERRA, and Young Living sell special blends for common problems including sore muscles, stress, sleeplessness, coughing/lung problems, and more. These can be a wonderful addition to your home medicine cabinet.

Aloe Vera

Although people do take aloe vera internally, the only uses discussed here are external. Internal use of aloe vera has very real risks and should not be done without trained medical supervision.

Aloe is a natural antiseptic. It can kill funguses, bacteria, viruses, and more. It is widely used for mild burns (first or second degree), such as sunburn or minor kitchen mishaps. It can help with insect stings and mild frostbite.

Activated Charcoal

Activated charcoal can be used to treat poisons and gas/bloating, among other things. It is similar to regular charcoal, but has been treated to be used as medicine and doesn't contain the additives barbeque charcoal commonly does. (In other words, no, you can't make your own and you can't use barbeque charcoal.)

Activated charcoal works by binding the poison to itself so the poison can then be safely flushed out of the body. It is easy to become dehydrated when taking activated charcoal, so be sure to drink lots of water.

Cayenne Pepper

The capsaicin in cayenne pepper has massive medicinal benefits, most of them from taking it internally. Used regularly, cayenne can help reduce blood pressure and aid with indigestion (gas pain).

Its amazing ability to prevent or even stop heart attacks has been documented. To stop a heart attack in progress, add 1 tsp to 1 cup warm water and drink, but **do not neglect calling 911 and getting medical treatment.**

Externally, cayenne can stop the bleeding from wounds. It is reputed to do the same internally, but that is a true medical emergency and requires a lot of training and experience to care for.

Chamomile

Chamomile tea is a well-known sleep aid. It also helps with relaxation and stress reduction. Chamomile can help heal burns and improve digestion, or as a compress for eye inflammation.

Epsom Salts

The most well-known use of Epsom salts is in a bath to ease discomfort from aching backs and muscles. Soaking in Epsom salts can reduce discomfort from strained and sprained muscles, and help with athlete's foot.

A solution of 2 tbsp. per cup of cold water can help with poison ivy, mosquito bites, and mild sunburn.

Honey

Honey is always tasty and sweet, but only raw (preferably local) honey has real health benefits. The biggest one is that it has antibacterial properties. Instead of putting alcohol or an over-the-counter medication on cuts and scrapes, try using honey. It works without the pain of alcohol and, unlike most medication, has a very long shelf life.

Honey also has a proven track-record relieving coughs, most popularly in a cup of hot lemon tea. (Drinking **pineapple juice** is another effective home remedy for coughing.) Taken regularly, it may also help with seasonal allergies and acid reflux.

If it crystallizes, reheat honey slowly and it will be like new again.

Honey should never be given to anyone under one year of age.

Oral Rehydration Solution

It's easy to make homemade oral rehydration solution to help someone who is dehydrated to rehydrate more quickly. Add 1/4 tsp. of salt and 3 tsp. of sugar to a half liter of water; that's the size of a standard, store-bought or machine-vended bottle of water.

Most places recommend using twice that amount, but the reality is that half liter bottles of water are extremely common and larger ones are not. If you can get the person to drink two bottles of water, each with salt and sugar (above) added, that is preferable.

This isn't necessary for anyone who is simply a bit thirsty. It may be a good idea for people who are have been sweating a lot and not drinking very much. It is definitely a good idea for anyone who has recently vomited a lot or had bad diarrhea.

Tea Tree Oil

This is less well-known in the United States, but it has a wide variety of health-care properties. It is primarily used either topically or inhaled as steam, *not* taken internally. Because of its anti-bacterial and anti-fungal properties, tea tree oil is effective against warts and other foot funguses, such as athlete's foot.

A few drops of tea tree oil added to shampoo makes a very effective lice treatment that doesn't small as nasty as commercial products and can also be used for an itchy scalp. It may also help treat acne.

Added to a warm bath, tea tree oil can help with muscle aches.

Turmeric

In western culture, turmeric is either not thought of or associated with curry. This Indian spice has tons of medicinal uses. Traditional uses include a variety of ailments resulting in mucus and post-nasal drip.

The simplest way to use this is by making a "golden tea." Recipes are easy to find online, but it is basically warm milk that has turmeric added while it is being heated on the stove top. Any kind of milk can be used–soy, almond, coconut, or cow milk, but coconut and cow milk are recommended the most often.

(Cold) Water

Run cold water over a fresh cut until the bleeding stops, then clean and bandage it.

Run cold water over a fresh burn to cool the skin. The next step is treating the area with aloe vera or Burn Gel.

Activity

Learn more about how to use one of these home remedies. Buy the herb and try using it next time someone needs it.

Quick Quiz

T/F Cayenne pepper can help with heart attacks (but don't skip the 911 call).

T/F Chamomile tea can help with insomnia.

T/F Warm baths with Epsom salts or tea tree oil can help with muscle aches.

T/F Honey is an herbal remedy that can be used on cuts and scrapes to prevent infection.

T/F Cayenne pepper on a wound may stop bleeding.

Resources

Articles

Aloe Vera Uses
http://www.webmd.com/vitamins-supplements/ingredientmono-607-ALOE.aspx?activeIngredientId=607&activeIngredientName=ALOE

Cayenne Pepper Uses
http://medplant.nmsu.edu/capsicum.shtm

Cayenne Pepper and Heart Attacks
http://www.shirleys-wellness-cafe.com/NaturalFood/Cayenne.aspx

Chamomile Uses
http://www.herbwisdom.com/herb-chamomile.html

Epsom Salts
http://www.saltworks.us/salt_info/epsom-uses-benefits.asp

Epsom Salts Bath
http://www.naturalnews.com/042753_Epsom_salt_baths_remarkable_health_benefits_detoxificatin_technique.html

CHAPTER NINETEEN

Honey Uses
http://www.webmd.com/diet/medicinal-uses-of-honey?page=2

Honey More Uses
http://www.medicalnewstoday.com/articles/264667.php

How to Use Activated Charcoal
http://wellnessmama.com/247/activated-charcoal/

Tea Tree Oil Uses
http://www.activistpost.com/2013/05/the-miracle-of-tea-tree-oil-80-amazing.html

Books

Aloe Vera Handbook: The Ancient Egyptian Medicine Plant by Max B. Skousen

*Cayenne Pepper Cures (Miracle Healers From The Kitchen) (Volume 1) by Sharon Daniels

The Independent Herbalist: A Beginner's Guide to Herbal Preparedness by Agatha Noveille

*A Kid's Herb Book: For Children of All Ages by Lesley Tierra

Maria's Mixes: A How-To Guide On Making Your Own Herbal Teas by Maria Yeager

Natural Bath Herb Recipes for a Relaxing Bath: Herbal Bath Teas, Bath Salts & Essential Oil Blends (Little Herb Books Book 1) by Terri Primavera

*Power Healers: Apple Cider Vinegar, Coconut Oil, Cayenne Pepper & Cinnamon Honey: Complete Collection Of Healing Remedies, Cures, & Recipes. Boost Immune Systems, Prevent Allergies & Help Lose Weight by Patricia Gardner

HOME REMEDIES

Water: For Health, for Healing, for Life: You're Not Sick, You're Thirsty! by F. Batmanghelidj

Other

Aloe Vera Gel

Cayenne Capsules

Cayenne Pepper

Chamomile Flowers

Tea Tree Oil

{Twenty}

Calling 911

When everything has truly gone catastrophically wrong, it's time to call for emergency services to help.

What number should you call?

Silly as that sounds, there really are different numbers. Most areas *in the United States* use 911 for Emergency Services, but not all do. In addition, if you are traveling, your cell phone may not call the closest emergency services if you simply dial 911.

If you are taking a cross-country road trip, listing every phone number along the way is unrealistic. Any time you are staying somewhere for more than a few days, you should check to confirm 911 is the right number, especially if you have someone who has serious health problems or is accident-prone with you.

Finally, 911 is for *emergency* services. If it isn't a true emergency, call the non-emergency number for police or ambulance services. What is the non-emergency number? Search for your county or city name plus "non-emergency number" and the answer should be at the top of your search results.

When should you call the emergency number?

911 is for on-going medical and police emergencies. If you get home to find your home trashed but have no reason to think the thief or vandal is still there, call the non-emergency number for your local police department. If you have reason to believe the person(s) is still in your home, you may be in danger and should call 911 immediately. Be sure to let them know the person may still be in the house.

If you arrive to visit an elderly relative and find her in bed, cold and dead, it's too late for anyone to help. This is another time to call the non-emergency number. But if you arrive to find her slumped over the table, unresponsive but alive, call 911 as fast as your fingers can dial.

What information do they need?

Type of Emergency

They need to know what kind of crew and how many people to send. If a burglar broke one of your windows and stole some jewelry, they will need fewer police on site than if you are hiding in a closet while a big scary person terrifies the rest of your family. Likewise, a suspicious spider bite will not require as rapid a response as a heart attack or stroke.

Knowing the kind of emergency also lets them tailor the advice they give you to the situation. When my grandmother had a massive stroke, the 911 dispatcher had us roll her onto the side because they knew she would throw up and that was the safest position to have her in when that happened.

Location/Address

They may be able to pull your location from the phone, but that really works best with landlines. They have a specific address attached to them and are always at that address.

If you are literally on the road, tell them the route you are on and if there are any cross-streets nearby. If there aren't any cross-streets nearby, any other identifying information will help them. If you just passed a large cattle farm or saw alpacas grazing, that might be just the information they need to pinpoint you.

If you are in a hotel, they will need the exact name of it and your room number. Since many hotels are large chains, simply saying you are at Hotel Buena Vista in Metropolis City may not help much because Metropolis is *big* and probably has several. If you say the Hotel Buena Vista Union Station Room 1313 or Hotel Buena Vista at the corner of Main and Market, now they can locate you exactly.

Once they know your location, stop talking and wait for any additional questions they ask.

Important Medical Information

They may not need this until medical assistance arrives, but they will need to know if anyone with you has any serious medical conditions or allergies, and they will need insurance information.

Most people keep insurance cards in their wallet or purse. Some also have pill boxes or have apps on their phone listing all their critical medical information such as their doctor's name and the pharmacy phone number.

What should you *not* do?

Try not to panic.

Don't talk over them, if you can help it. If your battery is about to die and you have to get some last important information out before that happens, tell them that ("My battery is about to die and I need to tell you...") and the information they need to know. Otherwise, they may be giving or requesting important information that you miss because you are talking.

Don't hang up until they tell you to.

Don't yell at them, unless they say the connection is bad and they can't hear you.

Don't get in their way once they arrive.

CHAPTER TWENTY

What other numbers might you need?

You need to have the non-emergency numbers for the local police and fire departments. You may have a separate sheriff's department as well.

If someone is injured, you will almost certainly need to have phone numbers for all that person's regular doctors and their pharmacy. They are probably in the contacts for their cell phone. Ask your parents to store this information in a way you can find it, even if that is a note that lists the names of their doctors.

If your guardian is injured, you need to know the name and phone number for another adult who can pick you up and watch you until they are released to come home. You may just know where to find it either written down or in a cell phone, but that will help you stay safe and with people you know and trust.

Letting Someone Inside

There is someone with a badge outside, but are they really a police officer? If you just called for their help, they probably are. If you didn't call, it's not unreasonable to be suspicious. You can call police dispatch (*not* 911) to confirm.

This step requires advanced preparation. Keep one or more house keys, each attached to a glow-stick, upstairs and easily accessible. If anyone becomes trapped upstairs and needs first responders (law enforcement, firefighters, medical help) to enter the house, toss the keys with the lit-up glow stick out the window. They can find the key more quickly that way and avoid breaking down your front door or windows, a repair bill your family will be stuck with, not the first responders.

If Anyone is Carrying

If anyone with you is carrying a weapon (concealed or open carry) and is injured or unconscious, an adult will need to know so someone can take responsibility for that weapon until the owner or another adult is able to reclaim it.

If a firearm or any other valuable possessions are taken away, be very sure to get some kind of receipt proving exactly what was taken and by whom so it can be reclaimed later.

Activity

Practice making a 911 call, ***but do not actually call 911***. Calling 911 when you don't have an actual emergency is a really bad idea and may even be a crime. Instead, pretend to call and have someone you know and trust pretend to be the 911 operator.

Practice making a call to the non-emergency number.

If anyone in your family regularly carries a firearm, make a plan for what to do in an emergency.

Quick Quiz

T/F   Always call 911 in an emergency.

T/F   Emergency operators can easily and quickly find your location from your cell phone.

T/F   Be prepared to tell them exactly what happened and where you are located.

T/F   Emergency responders will not need any additional medical information from you.

T/F   Police dispatch can confirm whether a person at your door claiming to be a police officer really is a police officer.

Resources

Articles

Calling Emergency Services
http://www.wikihow.com/Call-Emergency-Services

Emergency Phone Numbers
http://en.wikipedia.org/wiki/Emergency_telephone_number

*How to Call 911 Effectively
http://firstaid.about.com/od/callingforhelp/ht/06_Good911.htm

How to Use 911
http://kidshealth.org/kid/watch/er/911.html

*When to Call 911
http://www.911.gov/whencall.html

Books

Answering 911: Life in the Hot Seat by Caroline Burau

It's Time to Call 911: What to Do in an Emergency by Inc. Penton Oversees

{Part 5}
Miscellaneous Survival Skills

There are many kinds of survival skills. Some are only for the wilderness and emergencies, but many (like cooking, already discussed) are skills ordinary people use every day in life.

Sewing: Everyone should be able to make basic repairs to their clothing. Simple repairs such as sewing on buttons and patches, and repairing tears are covered.

If you don't think sewing counts as a survival skill, consider how things would go in the winter if your coat had a giant rip or a broken zipper, preventing you from closing it fully. Think about doing nearly anything if the sleeve of your shirt was ripped and kept getting in your way, or your ripped pants tripped you every other step.

Swimming and floating: Most of us already know how to swim (including doggy paddle), float, and tread water, but it's important and bears repeating. Dog paddling isn't pretty, but this is about survival, not qualifying for the Olympics. There are how-to videos for anyone who is still learning or needs a reminder.

This section also briefly discusses life-saving techniques for water rescues. That sounds complicated and kind of scary, but one of the most basic ones is holding out something for them to grab, like a stick or paddle, and then pulling the endangered swimmer to safety. That is neither complicated nor difficult.

Pack a survival pack: My kids packed their own packs, and they still can't remember most of what's in them. If you don't pack your own survival bag, there is zero chance you will remember what is in it, and only slightly more that you will remember how to use it.

After you pack it, go through it a few times a year to check everything is still good. Spring and fall are good times because you can swap out any seasonal items as well as checking expiration dates.

Safely use a knife: There are many kinds of knives, for many different uses. The two primary kinds most people use are kitchen knives and whittling knives. Choosing, carrying, caring for, and sharpening them are all covered.

Whittling knives are usually, but not always, pocketknives. There is a mind-blowingly large variety of these available, with all kinds of decorations on them. No matter what color, size (within reason—they are intended to fit in a pocket) or style you prefer, there is a pocketknife out there for you.

Kitchen knives just may be the hardest-working knives around. As with pocketknives, the variety available is astounding, but the reality is that most people only need a few.

No heat at home: It happens. Furnaces break. Fuel supplies run out.

Whatever the cause, there's no heat in the house and it's *cold* outside. Having a plan to handle the crisis can mean the difference between safety and comfort, and dangerous cold, or between staying home and a (possibly large) hotel bill.

React to Gunfire. There aren't many times when recognizing gunfire is a critical skill in most of our lives, but when it is critical, it is *really* critical.

It is also important to know what to do when you hear gunfire. It may be to run, but it may also be to hide. It is almost certainly best to remain quiet.

{Twenty-One}

Sewing

There is a reason soldiers, sailors, housewives, and just about anyone who needs to be self-sufficient has traditionally known how to do basic sewing and carried a simple sewing kit: **things always need to be made and repaired.**

Very few people need to be so good at sewing that they can take a few bolts of cloth, some sewing notions (needle, thread, etc.), and turn it into a perfectly fitted formal suit with no pattern. In fact, pretty much no one needs to be able to do that. Making simple items like a pencil case or a bag, and mending clothing that has a ripped seam or lost a button is another matter entirely. Everyone should be able to do those things.

Thread and Use a Needle

Find thread that matches what you need to sew. If it's a patch, match the color of the outside edge. If you don't have any that matches, go buy some. Fabric stores have hundreds of choices, so be sure to take the item to match it as closely as possible.

If the thread end is frayed, threading a needle is much harder. You can make the end wet and smooth down the end with your fingers to make it easier, or snip off the last little bit at an angle so it is smooth again. Then thread it through the eye of the needle. (Cutting it at an angle makes threading it easier.) If that is really hard, you may need a little gadget called a "needle threader."

Personally, I always make the ends on both sides of the eye of the needle the same length and tie a knot in the end. This leaves the thread doubled for hand-sewing, making everything I sew a bit more secure.

If you are afraid of tangling the thread, you may want to cut a shorter length of thread. You can also double the thread, being sure to pull the thread through carefully after each stitch. That will help prevent knots from forming or one end getting caught on something and forming a ball of stuck thread.

When you finish, knotting the thread up right against the fabric is the most common way to finish a hand stitched project. Another way is to sew several small stitches right over top of each other so the thread won't come out easily.

Sew on a Button

When you buy a new piece of clothing, it often comes with a small plastic bag with a spare button or two in it. For button-down shirts, the spare button may be sewn on the inside, below the last button, so it can't easily be lost. Find a small container that you won't easily lose and keep all those loose buttons in there. Whenever you lose a button, look there first for a replacement.

There are three basic kinds of buttons. One has a plastic loop at the back and the stitches are not seen, so it doesn't matter as much if they are neat. The others have two or four holes on the front and the stitches are seen.

For two-hole buttons, simply go through both, ending with the needle on the back of the fabric since that is where you left the knot when you started. Repeat the process until you have enough stitches to hold it secure, then knot off the end on the inside of the garment, where it can't be seen, and cut the thread.

For four-hole buttons, you can either have two sets of parallel stitches so the end result looks like an equal sign, or two sets that cross each other so the end result looks like an X. Either way, alternate which two holes you go through so there are equal numbers of stitches for all four holes. When it is secure, knot off the end and cut the thread.

Watch the video on sewing on a button in Resources for a more advanced technique to make your button-sewing slightly better.

Fix a Tear

There are lots of kinds of tears. Some aren't fixable, some are. It largely depends on the condition of the remaining fabric and the location. For many tears, an iron-on patch will suffice, although they can become loose after repeated washings if they aren't sewn on. These are readily available at fabric, pharmacy, and general merchandise stores.

If a pair of pants has a hole in the seat because they sat on something with a nail sticking out and that ripped a hole in otherwise-good-condition fabric, it's time for a repair. Many times, such as this, the two sides can be sewn together with a needle and thread and nothing more is needed. The fabric must be in good condition for this to work.

Other times, the rip isn't easily fixed. This happens most often when the fabric has become "threadbare." It is actually thinner than on other parts of the garment due to long, hard usage. If there is a tear in a threadbare of a section, it will need to be patched differently and with a larger patch. The patch needs to extend for *at least* an inch or so past the threadbare area to help keep it from tearing again soon.

There is a reason certain kinds of sports coats are sold with "patches" on the elbows: In the past, the elbows wore out very quickly and had to be patched, so now they just sell them with sturdier fabric there. The same principal applies to the jodhpurs horse riders wear. If a pair of pants has a hole in the seat because the fabric is worn through from heavy use, there really isn't much point in patching that area because you'll have to do it again fairly soon.

Sew on a Patch

Find or buy a thimble before you start. The thick material of patches can be hard to push a needle through and wearing a thimble helps, a lot. It also saves on the damage to your fingers, a lot.

There are two basic ways to sew on a patch. As with most hand sewing, start by making a knot on the inside where it can't be seen.

The first way is to have each stitch go from the inside over the edge, down through just the fabric, and back up through just inside the edge, repeating the process all the way around the edge of the patch. The second way is to have all of your stitches go through the fabric, just inside the outer edge.

The outer edges of decorative patches are always very thick from the thread wrapped around them, making sewing through them very tough. Some decorative patches have the entire inside embroidered as well, making them even more difficult to sew through, while others are either only partially embroidered or are printed on the center. Personal preference and how thick the center is will probably make your choice of which way to sew a patch on much easier.

Simple Items

Have you ever had a hard time finding exactly what you want for a simple fabric item? It could be a pencil pouch, a bag, a quilt, curtains, or even clothing like a robe or shorts. If you know how to sew, you can make your own, exactly the way you like it.

The first steps are deciding what you want and going to the store for fabric, if you don't already have it.

Start with something simple, like a pillowcase or a pencil bag. Select a fabric you like. For a pillowcase, you'll want something softer but fairly durable because it is used every day. For a pencil case, you'll simply need something very durable and thick enough that pencil points won't poke through and scissors (if you carry them) won't make a hole.

Many people have a collection of old t-shirts they love or that have special memories. These are a great candidate for a scrap quilt! A scrap quilt is pieces of scrap fabric sewn together into a quilt. Once you have them all sewn together, make another, equally sized piece that will be the back, and a third layer of filling (batting) to put in the middle. The filling helps it be a warmer, softer blanket.

Normally, you start by sewing all three layers together just at the edges, inside out. Leave a section on one edge unsewn and pull the whole thing though there so it is right side out, then hand sew that edge shut. Finish it by using a machine to sew a pattern across the whole thing that will keep the stuffing in place.

Activity

Find something that has a hole or missing button and repair it.

OR

Decide something you can use and make it.

CHAPTER TWENTY-ONE

Quick Quiz

T/F   There is only one right way to fix a ripped item.

T/F   There are several kinds of buttons.

T/F   Different items require different kinds of fabric and thread.

T/F   T-shirts can make a fun scrap quilt.

T/F   It is impossible to sew without a pattern.

Resources

Use discretion when choosing how early to teach children how to use sharp or otherwise potentially dangerous items.

Articles

About Sewing
http://sewing.about.com/

DIY Designs and Sewing Craft Ideas
http://www.favecrafts.com/Sewing

HGTV Sewing
http://www.hgtv.com/design/topics/sewing

Simplicity Sewing
http://simplicity.com/t-sewing-how-to.aspx

Books

My First Sewing Machine Book: Learn to Sew by Alison McNicol

A Kid's Guide to Sewing: Learn to Sew with Sophie & Her Friends 16 Fun Projects You'll Love to Make & Use by Sophie Kerr

Other

Needle Threader

Repair Badges (iron on)

Sewing Kit

Thimble

Scouting-Specific

Textile Artist Badge
http://forgirls.girlscouts.org/home/badgeexplorer/#textile-artist

Videos

Mend a Tear with Iron On Tape
https://www.youtube.com/watch?v=vx0TEhGnZcY

How to Sew on a Button - 5 Simple Steps - A Mans Guide to Sewing
Buttons on Shirts Jackets Trousers
https://www.youtube.com/watch?v=fu3F8GSK8DQ

How to Sew a Patch
https://www.youtube.com/watch?v=WzL1AEXAd7Y

{Twenty-Two}

Swimming and Floating

For survival purposes, the goal is simply to ensure you can survive. There is no need to have perfect form in the butterfly stroke, or to be able to dive in and swim the length of an Olympic pool in one breath. If you can manage to not go under in water over your head for five minutes, that's a great start, even if it's all dog-paddling.

Extra weight (heavy shoes, a coat, etc.) make it harder to stay afloat and to swim. In a situation where you know you are about to go in the water for an extended period of time (such as a boat sinking), evaluate what you may need to take off, how cold the water is, and if there is anything close enough to grab that may help you survive.

If there is a deck cushion/flotation device, a life preserver, or anything similar, it will allow you to conserve more of your energy and survive longer. It may also make it possible to shelter at least parts of your body from the sun and not be fully submerged for as long. Sunburn can be a very real danger, and the longer you are exposed, the worse it gets.

In addition, our body temperature is 98.6. Unless it is a hot spring or other unusual location, natural bodies of water are almost never that warm. This means they are cooler than a human body and will cool it off. Even somewhere relatively warm like the Caribbean, a person stuck in the water for too long can suffer from hypothermia. Figuring out a way to minimize your time in the water can be a matter of life or death.

Swimming and floating can't really be learned from a book. Luckily, swimming lessons are widely available at local pools, gyms, and all sorts of other locations. Give one a try!

Water hazards such as rip tides and currents are covered in *26 Outdoor Life Skills,* Book 3 of this series.

Floating

If you only learn one water-based skill, learn to float. Most people can float far longer than they can swim and this buys time for some-one to find and help you. It doesn't take much energy or skill, alt-hough some people are naturally more buoyant than others. That means their body floats closer to or at the surface of the water. Less buoyant people may float a few inches below the water.

The basic principal is to make your body cover as much area as pos-sible. To do this, put your arms straight out to your side so they make one continuous line across your body, like a T. Move your feet out as far as you comfortably can under that line, making an upside down V.

You have just made your body into a TV to float.

Arch your back to keep your stomach up toward the sky because the rest of your body will follow your stomach. If it stays up, you stay up. If it doesn't, you don't.

You can float on your stomach, but then you must turn your head to breathe regularly. Because of that, the back-float is far more common.

Swimming

You can spend years perfecting swimming technique and getting faster in the water, but the most important point, for this book is to know enough to not drown.

Keep your arms moving and legs kicking. Keep your head above water or remember to surface or turn your head to breathe.

When you are underwater, recognize the limits of your lungs. Don't stay under too long. Knowing how this feels is important because our lung capacity does vary a bit. Anyone who exercises a lot will improve their lung capacity, but something as simple as a head cold or hayfever can temporarily decrease it.

Treading Water

Like floating, treading water uses less energy than swimming. Treading water for increasingly longer periods of time is also a great way to build up endurance.

Put your arms out so they are on or near the surface of the water. If you have something to hold onto like a piece of wood or a life preserver, you can hold onto that instead. Kick with your legs. Your legs are straight under you, like you are standing. If you move them forward or back, you'll end up swimming instead.

To tread water, move your arms and legs back and forth. This will keep you from going under water. Your arms should stay on or near the surface of the water.

There are lots of specifics about how to tread water in the link in the Resources section, but if you simply get in water that is at least as deep as you are tall, then you can try and see what works for you. (Since your head will be out of the water, if the water is a deep as you are tall, you won't quite be able to touch the bottom and breathe at the same time.)

Life-Saving Techniques

If someone else is in the water and needs help, do you know how to give it to them? Without endangering yourself or anyone else?

Reaching

Simple enough: use something long and sturdy to reach a person who is a bit to far to reach otherwise. If you are in a canoe and someone falls overboard, hold out an oar toward them. Once they grab it, pull them toward you so they can climb back in. Poles of any sort (including fishing poles) and branches work too.

CHAPTER TWENTY-TWO

Rescue Craft

If someone is in the water and needs help but you're on the shore, you can use a boat, canoe, even a surfboard to help get them back to land.

Swim to Them

You may be able to swim out to a person who needs rescue, but be very careful so you don't end up needing rescued, too. You must be a strong enough swimmer, with enough strength and energy to reach them and come back with the weight of both of you. Very, very few people of any age or physical fitness level can manage that.

Throwing a Lifeline

Sometimes, the person is too far for reaching to work and there isn't a boat nearby. You need to throw a rope because it is easier to throw a rope a longer distance. It's obvious, but make sure to keep ahold of one end. The other end should be tied to something that floats like a life preserver or an air-filled jug. If it isn't, it will sink in front of the person you are trying to save, doing them no good.

Once they grab it or tie it around themselves, pull them toward safety. If you need help pulling them or something gets caught and you need help, don't be shy—ask for help. A person's life literally depends on it.

Activity

Go to a pool and practice the following:

- Dunking your head under water.
- Holding your breath under water, and knowing when it's time to come up because you reached the limit of your lungs for today.
- Pushing off from the wall and seeing how far you can go.
- Swimming any way you can, including doggy paddle, for as far as you can. If you can go four lengths of the pool–congrats! Even if it's not pretty, you're still a decent swimmer from a survival point of view.
- Try swimming underwater and see how far you can comfortably go.

Now go to a lake, pond, or ocean and try all of those again–making sure a life guard is nearby in case anything happens. Be very sure not to push yourself too far since open water is riskier than a pool. Tides, uncertain footing, murky water, floating debris (dead fish, plants), vegetation growing on the bottom and sides–all of these combine to make swimming more difficult than in a pool.

How was the natural body of water different than the pool? Which do you like more? How do you think an emergency like a flash flood or hurricane would affect lakes, rivers, ponds, the ocean, etc.? How would that affect how long you can do the activities listed above?

Quick Quiz

T/F   Holding out an oar to reach a swimmer in trouble is one life-saving technique.

T/F   Dog-paddling isn't swimming.

T/F   If your whole body isn't on the surface of the water, then you aren't floating.

T/F   Swimming uses less energy than floating.

T/F   There is more than one way to swim.

Resources

Articles

Treading Water
http://www.wikihow.com/Tread-Water

Books

Learn to Swim: Even if You are Terrified (Swimming Book 1) by Michele McGrath

Learn to Swim: Teaching You to Teach Your Child to Swim by Benjamin Roberts

Teach Yourself to Swim Like a Pro: In One Minute Steps by Dr. Pete Anderson

Other

Instructional Swim Belt - Three Module

Swim Vest (Coast Guard Approved)

Scouting-Specific

LifeSaving Merit Badge
http://meritbadge.org/wiki/index.php/Lifesaving

Swimming Merit Badge
http://meritbadge.org/wiki/index.php/Swimming

Water Sports Merit Badge
http://meritbadge.org/wiki/index.php/Water_Sports

Videos

How to Help Children Learn to Swim-video
https://www.youtube.com/watch?v=8oi7vTUtu3I

How to Learn Swimming
https://www.youtube.com/watch?v=WreddX9aeGw

How to Tread Water for Beginning Swimmers
https://www.youtube.com/watch?v=kFmOtf_Ew1w

Swimming Tips: How to Float on Your Back
https://www.youtube.com/watch?v=vhtpckfbxp0

{Twenty-Three}

Survival Packs

The only want to really know what is in a bag–any bag–is to be the one to pack it. That most definitely includes survival packs.

Survival packs should be tailored for their user and the use. A school survival bag, a car survival bag, a winter survival bag, a summer survival bag, a vacation survival bag–each of these should be slightly different. A bag for an infant, a school age child, a teen, a grandparent, a man, a woman, a pet (yes, pets need them too), a classroom, or even visiting guests are still more ways survival packs may need differentiated.

For all those individual differences, there are many more similarities in what needs to be included. A survival pack is a bag full of items, including food and either water or a water purification system, to help the user survive in an emergency. The basics also include a first aid kit, tools, emergency blankets, and a small, light-weight form of entertainment, such as a deck of cards.

First Aid Kit

There are lots of different kinds of first aid kits, in all kinds of sizes. For school, pack a first aid kit without any actual medication or pointy objects of any kind, like tweezers. Those make school officials unhappy, if they find them at school.

The truth is that the first thing to go bad in any first aid kit is the medicine. Bandages, gauze, splints, braces, and just about anything else is good for decades. Besides, handing out medicine is best done by an adult. This has nothing to do with skill and everything to do with The Rules and what will make administrators and other adults unhappy.

The most basic items to include are bandages and something to prevent infection. Raw (usually local) honey is perfect for this, and you can store the small amount needed for this in a contact lens case without having to worry about leaks. You can put aloe for burns in the other side of the case. In both cases, only a small amount is needed on the affected area.

Other possible items include:

- Popsicle stick: finger splint.
- Lanyard: makeshift sling.
- Travel size soap containers: hold bandages and other small items.
- Mylar emergency blanket.
- EMT shears (small size).

The key point is to include items *you* can use and may need. Personalize the contents! Everyone in my family has something to combat motion sickness because even the dog gets car sick, but most people don't need that. Other people have epi-pens. Scout kits have moleskin because they hike a lot

Food and Water

Include enough snacks and water to last for a day or so. It can't be junk food, but it needs to be something you like to eat that will last for months because really, what is the chance that you will replace it more often than that? Bars are good, but chocolate ones will melt in the summer heat.

Also include water purification tablets and/or another way to purify water for drinking.

Tools

More than many other items, tools require skill. Don't carry tools you don't have the skill to use. EMT shears are the one simple tool that even really little kids can safely handle, thanks to the specially designed ends. In addition to quickly cutting off all kinds of clothing, they can cut through car seat belts and are great for cutting off wrist bands from theme parks, laser tag games, etc.

Small knives, multi-tools, and even household tools like a screwdriver, hammer, or wrench can be helpful addition, but be sure to learn how to safely use any tools you add and that you don't take anything to school that could cause trouble. Small folding shovels, also called "e-tools" are handy, but a bit heavy. (E-tool is short for "entrenching tool" because soldiers used them to dig trenches.) This makes them a good choice to keep in a vehicle.

Other Survival Items

Silver Mylar <u>emergency blankets</u> are a standard item, but if you have space, a wool emergency blanket is really a great addition. It is far harder to rip wool than Mylar and wool keeps the user warm even when it's wet. If you combine the two, it should keep you toasty warm.

A <u>sturdy whistle</u> is important. Everyone's voice gives out after enough yelling. Blowing on a whistle takes far less energy and doesn't require your voice to still be in good condition. If you are lost or stuck and need to be found, a whistle could save the day.

There are several kinds of <u>compasses</u>. If you really have no idea where you are or where you want to go, a compass won't help much. If you generally know where you need to head or have a map to help, it could be a big help.

<u>Extra (wool) socks</u> and a <u>hoodie</u> are good ideas. Wet or cold feet suck. A nice, clean pair of socks can do a lot to make anyone feel better. A hoodie is one extra layer to help you stay warm, and the hood keeps wind from blowing down your collar.

If you're stuck somewhere, unable to leave safely for hours or even days, a deck of playing cards or other simple, flexible game could be a huge boredom-buster and stress-reducer.

CHAPTER TWENTY-THREE

Activity

Find an empty bag or backpack and build your own survival bag. Have an adult review it to see what you may have missed.

Quick Quiz

T/F   Some items need changed out periodically because they expire or heat exposure affects them, such as in a car trunk in the summer.

T/F   Wet wool blankets and socks still keep people warm.

T/F   Whistles are useless in a survival situation.

T/F   If you include water, then you don't need a way to purify water.

T/F   Knowing how to use any tools in your emergency bag is important.

Resources

Articles

*Choosing and Packing Your Kids' Emergency Bag
http://momprepares.com/choosing-and-packing-your-kids-emergency-bag-what-to-bring/

Deconstructing the Emergency Bag
http://www.treehugger.com/culture/deconstructing-the-emergency-bag-packing-a-kit-is-tougher-than-it-looks.html

How to Pack an Emergency Bag
http://www.wikihow.com/Pack-an-Emergency-Bag

Packing an Emergency Bag
http://thesurvivalmom.com/packing-an-emergency-kit/

Books

Bug Out Bag: Disaster Survival Guide For Beginning Preppers by Miles Bennett

Build the Perfect Bug Out Bag: Your 72-Hour Disaster Survival Kit by Creek Stewart

*Emergency Bag Essentials (Swatchbook): Everything You Need to Bug Out by Jason Charles

Realistic Bug Out Bag by Max Cooper

Scouting-Specific

Emergency Preparedness Merit Badge
http://meritbadge.org/wiki/index.php/Emergency_Preparedness

Videos

Extended Travel Emergency Bag (for cars/trucks)
https://www.youtube.com/watch?v=WS6W2Mv9Bo0

Joe Selwood learns to pack in an emergency kit (fire)
https://www.youtube.com/watch?v=eZo-AJKvyyY

*Emergency Preparedness: How to Pack a Survival Kit in Case of Emergency (for weather emergencies)
https://www.youtube.com/watch?v=GK0AjnRvNRU

{Twenty-Four}

Safe Knife Use

Blood Circle and Safety

The risk of injury will never be zero when a blade is in use, but it can be minimized with a little care and thought.

Take your *closed* knife in your hand and spin in a circle. That is your blood circle. Anyone within that distance of you risks having their blood drawn by your knife because they are dangerously close.

When a knife isn't in use, it should always be closed and put away somewhere safe. If it needs cleaned before being closed, take the time to clean it before someone is injured. If that is impossible for some reason, find somewhere safe and secure to store it.

Always cut with the blade going down and away from your body. That way, if the blade slips, the risk of a serious injury is far less.

When carrying a bladed item, hold the handle, face the blade out (away from your body) with the point aimed down at the ground.

Carrying

Carrying a knife is a right that needs to be earned. Until then, an adult needs to keep the knife until and unless it is being used. Once you can carry it yourself, pocketknives can be kept in a pocket or in a sheath. Sheath knives are normally carried in a sheath. Simply put, different kinds of knives can be carried in different ways, but the blade should always be covered when not in use.

If the blade can be closed, then close it. If it has a sheath, put it back in the sheath. Then hand you can walk around with it or hand it to another person. Do not walk around with an open, unsheathed knife, and don't hand it to another person. Opening and closing/sheathing and unsheathing only takes a moment, but it keeps other people safe and keeps your blade in better condition. How? You are less likely to drop it or hit something by accident, nicking or otherwise damaging the blade.

Cleaning

Before putting away any blade, up to and including swords, the blade must be clean. If it is not clean, any residue on it will get inside where the blade is stored (sheath, scabbard, or the inside of a folding knife, it doesn't matter). Once it's there, removal will be nearly impossible. That residue may cause damage for a long time.

If there is sap, food residue (including blood, bits of meat from dinner, jelly, *anything)*, or anything else potentially sticky, it significantly increases the chance of rust or other damage to the metal. So just clean it promptly. That also makes it easier to put away safely promptly.

Oil the blade regularly to ensure a long life and smooth, safe operation.

Kitchen Use

In addition to the safety rules above, there are a few more when you are working with food in a kitchen. The first is to use a cutting board, possibly even two or three (Chapter 13: Food Safety). That reduces the chances of injury.

Use the correct knife for the job. There is a reason for every kind of kitchen knife. Start by learning their names because those are a good clue to their purpose. A bread knife is for...cutting bread. A steak knife is ideal for cutting steak. A basic cutting block has five knives and a sharpener. Learn how to use those basic knives properly.

Never leave a sharp knife somewhere hidden, like lying in a container of soapy water. Someone could be injured. Putting them away properly doesn't take that long.

Selecting a Knife

There are tens of thousands of choices of knives. The first step is deciding how and where the knife will be used. A whittling knife is different than a knife for cleaning fish which is different than a butcher knife.

Personal fit and carrying preferences also affect knife choice. A smaller hand will always be more comfortable with a smaller knife than a large hand will be. A sheath knife is ill suited to a person who plans to carry their knife in a pocket.

An "automatic" knife is similar to a switchblade. In many areas, they are only available to Law Enforcement Officers and the military. They are not appropriate for youth.

The most common first knife is a folding knife. More specifically, a pocketknife. They are often used for whittling and other small jobs.

Sheath blades are generally fixed blades. A fixed blade doesn't fold in any way. A sheath blade is one that is held in a sheath. These are generally larger, longer blades. Sheath blades can be used for larger tasks, such as cutting small limbs off of trees.

Sharpening

In addition to being clean, blades need to be sharp. Because a dull knife requires more pressure to cut, a dull blade is more likely to cause an injury than a sharp one. There are videos in the Resources section to demonstrate sharpening techniques.

According to FamilyHandyman.com:

> You can sharpen most garden tools with a simple 10-in. mill bastard file. A synthetic finishing stone will further smooth the

blade edge, which is important, especially on an ax or hatchet. You can get one at any hardware store. You don't need a fancy Arkansas stone for garden tools.

If you read that article, you will see that there are many different ways to sharpen a blade, and many different kinds of blades that need to be sharpened, but the basic principles are the same for them all. No matter how you do it, knives must be clean before being sharpened.

The basic technique involves sliding the edge (but *never* the blade) across a rough surface, such as ridged steel or ceramic, to make it smooth, just as wood becomes smooth after being sandpapered. The rough surface can be metal or ceramic.

One of the oldest known ways is using a whetstone. There are more modern variations available, but the technique is the same. A whetstone needs to be wet. When you put it in water, no bubbles should come out. If they do, leave it soak for a few more minutes. More modern versions do not have to be soaked but they either need oil or result in a rougher final product.

Rub the blade back at a 10-30° angle, depending on the blade's original angle. Be sure to apply even pressure and move quickly. Either flip it from one side to the other as you work, or when one side is finished, flip it over and sharpen the other side.

A honing rod is another tool. It is used almost the same way, except that it is a rod held in your hand instead of a block setting on the table. Honing is more of a maintenance activity for a relatively sharp knife. True sharpening is needed for really dull blades.

Activity

Find a stick to use for cooking a hot dog or marshmallow. Remove all the bark from the end and sharpen it into a point to stick the food onto. When you are finished, clean your knife and put it safely away.

Green wood usually works best for this because it won't catch fire as easily as drier wood.

Quick Quiz

T/F   It is safe to be halfway inside someone else's blood circle.

T/F   Blades may be put away dirty if they are cleaned within two days.

T/F   There are multiple ways to sharpen a blade.

T/F   A lot of choosing a knife comes down to personal preference.

T/F   Knowing how you plan to use it is part of choosing a knife.

Resources

Use care when choosing to teach anyone how to use sharp or otherwise potentially dangerous items.

Articles

FamilyHandyman.com:
http://www.familyhandyman.com/tools/how-to-sharpen-tools/view-all

Safe Kitchen Knife Use
http://www.nfsmi.org/documentlibraryfiles/PDF/20110314110311.pdf

CHAPTER TWENTY-FOUR

Types of Kitchen Knives
http://www.recipetips.com/kitchen-tips/t--1075/types-of-kitchen-knives.asp

Folding Knife Safety Rules
http://www.coastportland.com/articles/folding-knife-safety-rules-for-kids/

How to Sharpen a Knife
http://www.wikihow.com/Sharpen-a-Knife

Books

An Edge in the Kitchen: The Ultimate Guide to Kitchen Knives -- How to Buy Them, Keep Them Razor Sharp, and Use Them Like a Pro by Chad Ward

Complete Starter Guide to Whittling: 24 Easy Projects You Can Make in a Weekend (Best of Woodcarving) by the Editors of Woodcarving Illustrated

How To Sharpen A Knife & Care For Your Collection by James Morgan Ayres

Other

Lansky Ceramic Sharp Stick (Honing Rod)

Winco Sharpening Steel

Nite Ize Holster (knife sheath)

Whetstone Cutlery Two-Sided Whetsone

Scouting-Specific

Totin' Chip (safe use of pocket knives, axes, and hatchets)
http://meritbadge.org/wiki/index.php/Totin%27_Chip

Whittlin' Chip (safe use of pocket knives)
http://meritbadge.org/wiki/index.php/Whittlin%27_Chip

Wood Carving Merit Badge
http://meritbadge.org/wiki/index.php/Wood_Carving

Woodworker Badge
http://forgirls.girlscouts.org/home/badgeexplorer/#woodworker

Videos

Choosing a Knife for Camping - a Beginners Guide
https://www.youtube.com/watch?v=Huv2s3cuKSE

How to Sharpen a Knives - Jamie Oliver's Home Cooking Skills (honing rod)
https://www.youtube.com/watch?v=oIz8QNVb4P8

How to Use a Sharpening Stone | Knives (whetstones)
https://www.youtube.com/watch?v=lBXRkMZfIXk

{Twenty-Five}

No Heat at Home

What will you do if the heat goes out in your home in the middle of the winter? Since that has happened to us several times (we have a new furnace now), we definitely have plans and materials if it happens again.

Having air conditioning go out is uncomfortable and inconvenient, but in most places, it's not really dangerous because it doesn't get or stay much more than *at most 20°F above* what is comfortable for humans. Cold is a different matter. Depending on where you live, it could be *far more than 40°F below* what is comfortable for humans for months during the winter.

I live in an area that definitely has a mild/moderate climate, and even here we've had times when you could get frostbite if you were outside and exposed for a mere 30 minutes. There can also be property damage, such as frozen pipes, at those temperatures.

Electricity is Still On

A year or two ago, the winter was so severe that there were propane shortages. Sometimes a scheduled delivery gets missed. Or perhaps the furnace is just broken. Whatever the reason, you realize the house is getting a bit nippy and when you check the thermostat, the heat isn't working–but the electricity is still on. That gives you more options than you have if it isn't, such as picking up the phone and calling for an HVAC repairman. If you don't have power, your landline may not work, especially if it's actually a voice over IP line through your cable company.

Since heating one room is far easier than heating a whole house, choose one room and focus on it.

- **Size**: The larger the room, the longer it will take to heat and the more energy it will take to heat it, but everyone needs to fit in.
- **Family size**: How many people will be in the room? If you need to fit eight people in, you'll need more space than if you need to fit three.
- **Outside openings**: The more doors and windows a room has, the more cold outside air is likely to seep in.
- **Interior openings**: Open doorways and pass-throughs need covered to keep the heat in. The more openings a room has, the more work sealing it off to keep it warm will be.
- **The actual space**: Your bathroom may be the best room looking at the above, but do you *really* want to

spend a day or more hanging out in there? As a family?

When this happened to us last year, we used our TV room. It has a big, comfy sofa, a TV with DVD player, and space on the floor for my kids to play. There are two internal doorways and two windows with thermal curtains, and it's about a 15x15 room. 15x15 is big enough for us to all fit comfortably, but small enough to heat quickly and keep warm easily with an electric space heater.

There aren't many interior doors on the first floor, just empty doorways, and none in this room. Clearly, the openings need closed to keep the heat in, but only temporarily.

I covered each entryway with a cheap silver emergency blankets and used packing tape to seal the edges to the walls to keep the heat in. One was taped closed all the way around. The second had one side free for entry and exit.

We could have used regular blankets instead of emergency blankets, but it would have been *far* harder to secure them on the walls because they weigh so much more. With a space heater on, the silver blankets seemed to do a good job of reflecting the heat back in and the room got nice and toasty.

As well as this worked, there are two improvements I will make if we ever have to do it again. First and foremost, put a blanket on each side of the doorway. Just as layers of clothing or glass on a double paned window have an insulating layer of air, this will create an insulating layer for the doorways. Second, there are zippers you can buy for just this sort of situation. They create doorways in a big sheet of plastic (Visqueen). One of those would have been very nice to have.

In the smaller bathroom, a little space heater designed to go under an office desk provided welcome warmth. For safety reasons, it could only be turned on when we were in the room, so we kept the bathroom doors shut to help the room stay warm.

Electricity is Out

If the electricity is out, an electric space heater is no longer an option. You will still need to choose a room and close it off to keep the heat in, but you really need to make sure there is a fireplace or something similarly non-electric in the room to heat it.

If you use something freestanding like a kerosene heater, please be *extremely* careful of fumes, as well as the possibility of knocking it over or bumping it and getting burned. These should only be operated by an adult and only with great care.

Activity

Turn the heat down low in your home and practice sealing up one room and spending the day in there. Don't try this when it is truly arctic outside because your furnace will have to work very hard to reheat your home. Try it when it is cold, but not below freezing in the daytime.

OR

Seal up one room in your house. Open the windows to the outside to let that room, and only that room, get cold. Then shut the windows and try reheating it as if the furnace wasn't working.

Quick Quiz

T/F Just choose the room with the most natural sunlight.

T/F Whether you have electricity or not, you will do the same things to keep warm in your home without a furnace.

T/F A working fireplace can be helpful when the furnace is out.

T/F Opening the doorway (curtain) between the warm room and the cold house a lot is a great way to keep the room warm.

T/F The only thing to consider when picking a room to heat is how big it is.

Resources

Articles

Power Outage Safety
http://www.redcross.org/prepare/disaster/power-outage

What You Need to Know When the Power Goes Out Unexpectedly
http://www.bt.cdc.gov/disasters/poweroutage/needtoknow.asp

What to Do if the Power Goes Out in the Winter
http://www.consumerenergycenter.org/tips/winter_lightsout.html

Books

When the lights go out!: A guide to living in your home without power or water, during a emergency by Dana G.

Other

Emergency Mylar Blankets

Tarp Zipper Door

Visqueen

{Twenty-Six}

React to Gunfire

Recognizing the sound of gunfire and knowing what to do if you hear it isn't important very often in most of our lives, but if it does become important, it will be critical.

If someone is shooting, you want not be where the bullets are headed. If you don't know where the shooting is coming from or it is clearly headed for you, then you need cover. **Cover means something to protect you** and is different than concealment. **Concealment just means you are hidden.** A blanket can conceal you, but it won't stop a bullet so it isn't cover. Hiding behind a reinforced concrete wall can do both.

Listen to the sound of gunfire online. (links in Resources.) As you can see from that single list, there are many kinds of weapons that make many different sounds. Those are all gunfire. The sound of a car backfiring is similar, but different.

Most of us will never memorize all of them, but having an idea of the differences is still good. And the truth is that most of us can recognize a few differences already, from having watched TV and movies. A machine gun is a very different threat from a revolver, which is different from a shotgun. (Because of the way revolvers and shot guns are made, they are not high-capacity weapons.)

Most of us have heard the rapid fire of a shot gun and the distinctive sound of a pump-action shot gun often enough on TV to recognize the basic idea. Clearly, their prime goal is entertainment and not accuracy, but few of us will ever be in a position where we need to identify the exact weapon the person shooting at us is using. Civilians simply don't need to know that.

Recently, there was a shooting on a French train. Several American soldiers were in the car he chose to start his attack. When the slide on his weapon stuck, they attacked and took him down. Being able to listen and identify that change in sound saved lives.

Lockdown

Today, most schools have lockdown drills and some offices do as well. If yours does not, take the time to look around and figure out what you would do if there was a shooter in the building.

A lockdown drill is different from fire and other evacuation drills because those teach everyone how to leave the building in a quick and orderly fashion. They presuppose that outside is safer than inside. Like a tornado drill, a lockdown drill is designed to keep students inside in the safest possible location.

In a lockdown drill, the goal is to prevent the shooter from either seeing or targeting you. Keeping them from entering any space they aren't already in is an important goal. Any doors that can be locked, will be locked if they aren't already. The people in those rooms will then hide so they can't be seen through the doors.

- Close and lock the doors, if they aren't already.
- Turn off the lights.
- Close any curtains or window blinds/shades.
- If the door has a window or there are other uncovered windows, cover them if it can be done quickly and safely.
- If there is an area that offers cover, move as many people as possible there.
- If there is nowhere with cover, move somewhere concealed from view from the windows and doors, or at the very least from the door.
- Everyone must stay out of the line of sight from the door from the time the incident starts until it ends.

Most people do not do lockdown drills at home, but it isn't a bad idea. The truth is that most of us are perfectly safe in our own homes, but being prepared is never a bad thing.

Cover and Concealment

Not everything can provide cover, and some things that provide cover have other disadvantages. In particular, anything brittle could send chips flying all over the place, potentially injuring anyone near by.

Bricks and tile are common building materials that can chip when hit.

True cover–something that can stop a bullet–is rare in most of our live. The engine block of car or truck, jersey barriers, and concrete columns are the most common ones in regular American life. Most homes are something called "stick construction." That means they are framed with wood, which is then covered by drywall and other materials. None of them provide cover. Some are made of stone or brick and those do provide better cover, but it's still not great.

The bottom line is that while you should look for cover in an emergency, you will almost certainly have to make due with concealment. Concealment is what kept an entire classroom of kindergartners alive during the Sandy Hook killings. The killer didn't see them so he didn't shoot them.

Don't think concealment is valueless because it doesn't protect you from bullets. It's better to never have them shoot at you at all than for them to try and miss. Concealment saves lives.

Acting and Reacting

The difference between acting and reacting is that acting is more controlled. When people act, they have most often had at least a small amount of time to think about what they are doing and decide if it is the best choice. Sometimes they have had days, weeks, months, or even years to consider their actions.

Reacting is generally an immediate response. There is no time to think or evaluate. That makes it easier to make mistakes, and harder to find the best response. If you can force yourself to stay calm, think before you act, and consider possible consequences before you act instead of rushing to do something–anything!–the final result will be better. This is true whether you are talking about an active shooter situation or getting caught breaking house or school rules.

Like any other skill, practice, practice, practice to get good at this. If you make a habit of slowing down and thinking before reacting when you are caught in small things like lying about whether you or your sister finished the last piece of pie or when you actually turned in a homework assignment, it will be easier to do when it's something bigger, like staying out past curfew and getting grounded, or even being pulled over by the cops for it. If you have a good reason, stay calm, and explain it, you may not get in trouble at all. No matter how good your reason, if you panic and get angry with your parents/a cop, it will make things worse. If you can stay calm when an authority figure gets really mad (no matter how unfair it seems), it will be easier to stay calm if you are ever in a truly life-or-death situation. Practice, practice, practice.

Make a list of any place you go every week–clubs, church, school, sports, family, friends, home. If you were there, where could someone attack from? How would you get out if there was a fire, earthquake or other emergency? Doors are the most probable place for a threat to enter and for you to exit, followed by windows. Where could you find cover or concealment? Where would you go to be safe when you left? Think about this for each place.

Mentally rehearse this plan whenever you go there. If you are at a restaurant or theater or somewhere else, think about these same things. The more you do this, the easier it will be. It will become second nature. Eventually, you will automatically note all the exits and cover in a room, and the best way for you to reach them.

Thinking about what will happen if something bad happens doesn't mean anything bad will happen. Everyone has fire drills and bus evacuation drills, but do you know anyone who has had a fire in their school or had to evacuate a bus due to an emergency? This is the same thing. It is learning to be prepared.

Activity

From where you are *right now*, find cover as quickly as you can. If there is no cover around, what would you do if shots really were ringing out near you? Sitting in my house right now, there isn't any cover nearby. My best choices would be to run into the basement (underground) or upstairs to hide in the bathtub. Neither one is very good cover or close by, but it's far better than a wall made out of drywall or regular furniture.

Quick Quiz

T/F   Different guns and ammo can change the sound of gunfire.

T/F   Surroundings affect how gunfire sounds.

T/F   A car backfiring can initially be mistaken for a gunshot.

T/F   Cover and concealment are the same thing.

CHAPTER TWENTY-SIX

T/F   Most bullets can easily pierce drywall and furniture.

Resources

Articles

Online Discussion re: Recognizing the Sound of Gunfire
http://thefiringline.com/forums/showthread.php?t=370736

React to Gunfire
http://www.wikihow.com/React-to-Gunfire

Recognize the Sound of Gunfire
http://www.activeresponsetraining.net/recognizing-the-sound-of-gunfire

Books

Staying Alive: How to Act Fast and Survive Deadly Encounters by Safe Havens International

Scouting-Specific

Rifle Merit Badge
http://meritbadge.org/wiki/index.php/Rifle_Shooting

Shotgun Merit Badge
http://meritbadge.org/wiki/index.php/Shotgun_Shooting

Videos

*KCK mom teaches kids to prepare for drive-by shootings
https://www.youtube.com/watch?v=er6jGx-U9fM

Answer Key

Chapter 1.

1. F

2. T

3. T

4. F

5. F

Chapter 2.

1. F

2. F

3. T

4. F (MOMs have maiden names)

5. T

Chapter 3.

1. F

2. T

3. F

4. F

5. F

Chapter 4.

1. T

2. F

3. F

4. F

5. F

Chapter 5.

1. T

2. T

3. T

4. F

5. F

Chapter 6.

1. F

2. T

3. F

4. T

5. F

Chapter 7.

1. F

2. T

3. F

4. T

5. F

Chapter 8.

1. F

2. F

3. T

4. F

5. F

Chapter 9.

1. F

2. F

3. F

4. T

5. T

Chapter 10.	Chapter 13.	Chapter 16.
1. T	1. T	1. T
2. T	2. F	2. T
3. T	3. T	3. T
4. T	4. F	4. T
5. T	5. F	5. F
Chapter 11.	Chapter 14.	Chapter 17.
1. T	1. T	1. F
2. T	2. F	2. T
3. F	3. T	3. F
4. F	4. F	4. T
5. T	5. T	5. T
Chapter 12.	Chapter 15.	Chapter 18.
1. F	1. T	1. F
2. T	2. T	2. F
3. F	3. T	3. T
4. T	4. F	4. T
5. T	5. T	5. T

Chapter 19.

1. T

2. T

3. T

4. T

5. T

Chapter 20.

1. F

2. F (usually, not always)

3. T

4. F

5. T

Chapter 21.

1. F

2. T

3. T

4. T

5. F

Chapter 22.

1. T

2. F

3. F

4. F

5. T

Chapter 23.

1. T

2. T

3. F

4. F

5. T

Chapter 24.

1. F

2. F

3. T

4. T

5. T

Chapter 25.

1. F

2. F

3. T

4. F

5. F

Chapter 26.

1. T

2. T

3. T

4. F

5. T

About the Author

Bethanne Kim's mom took her to Brownies when she was six and she has been motivated to Be Prepared ever since. The importance of being prepared for emergencies hit home after she moved to Los Angeles. Earthquake preparedness is important there for obvious reasons. That was shortly after a boil-all-water alert in the city she lived in before that and she worked in Florida shortly after a major hurricane wreaked havoc, so she made sure her family earthquake kits (car, home, work, and school) were always up to date.

Her family moved to the Eastern Megalopolis about the time the "prepper" movement really started. After years of hearing the importance of earthquake preparedness on top of years of Scouting's "Be Prepared", this idea really hit home for Kim and she started following The Survival Mom's website. Shortly after that, she started writing for it and became active again as a Scout leader.

As a mom, Kim thinks about preparedness differently than she did before kids. It's all well and good to think you are prepared because you have some MREs on hand, but can you get the family to actually eat them? With all the options available, why not make sure you can truly enjoy your emergency rations if you ever need to eat them? And why not us them on hikes and other outings, or even evenings when you don't have the time or energy for more than boiling some water?

Most preppers are ordinary people with ordinary lives and ordinary jobs, living in ordinary neighborhoods, who strive to be prepared for whatever hard times life throws at them by setting aside money, food, and other basic supplies so they have them in an emergency. While this can include big, scary apocalyptic events like an EMP or zombies, mostly it means "everyday" emergencies like blizzards (power outages), hurricanes (evacuation), the car breaking down on an isolated road, and job loss. (Job loss=no money for food, electricity, etc., especially if you are unprepared.)

Another part of preparedness is being able to do things yourself, without calling in a specialist. Growing your own herbs and vegetables, and building the greenhouse for them, are perfect examples of this. Knowing basic first aid and simple home remedies (possibly using herbs from your garden) to reduce doctor trips is another.

All of this led Kim to start writing books on emergency preparedness with the hope of helping even more normal families integrate preparedness into their lives, and to help kids develop important life skills as diverse as situational awareness and measuring for cooking. Her hops is that this series of books will help others see that basic preparedness isn't rocket science. Our grandparents and great-grandparents had and used these skills, after all.

Other Books

The Constitution: It's the OS for the US explains the historical context for the US Constitution and describes how it works using computer terms like firewall and plug-ins, not legalese. (An OS is a computer Operating System, like iOS for Apple devices.) It has questions for the reader about how they think the government should work rather than trying to persuade them to believe what the writer believes.

Survival Skills for All Ages Book 2: 52⁺ Recipes for Everyday & Emergencies is full of simple recipes that can be cooked on or off-grid, so you can serve normal meals even without power, and recipes for staples such as mayonnaise, baking powder, and crackers.

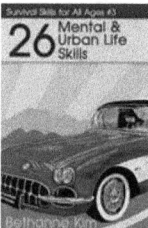

Survival Skills for All Ages Book 3: 26 Mental & Urban Life Skills covers financial skills, staying safe while traveling, self-defense, cyber security, hiding from danger, handling your emotions (including stress and anger), and more. These skills can help kids and adults throughout life, not just in emergencies.

Cubmastering: Getting Started as Cubmaster is an introduction for new Cubmasters. Topics covered include organizational structure, training, recruiting, and recharter. This is about more than just the nuts and bolts of Scouting, though. It also covers dealing with difficult parents and planning special pack events.

Scout Leader: An Introduction to Boy Scouts focuses on the nuts and bolts of Cub Scouts. Unit organization and BSA organization are both explained, as is recharter and the common BSA meetings (such as Roundtable) and trainings. Each chapter starts with a quote from Lord Baden Powell.

Citizenship in the World: Teaching the Merit Badge is, quite simply, a guide to assist merit badge counselors in teaching the BSA Eagle-required merit badge "Citizenship in the World." It includes the merit badge requirements, and information and tips for teaching it.

The Organized Wedding: Planning Everything from Your Engagement to Your Marriage is chock full of checklists. No detail is too small! What truly sets it apart is including the actual wedding ceremony and a chapter on your marriage with questions on financial priorities, family health history, and all your doctors.

OMG! Not the Zombies! Book 1 A group of teens goes for a hike and accidentally starts the zombie apocalypse. Being good at being prepared, they start setting up a safe community in the old Indian cliff houses and stocking it with supplies to save themselves and their families while the adults are still pretending life is normal.

BRB! Not the Zombies! Book 2 As their group grows, they discover a new mission: Get crucial information and items to the CDC to help with efforts to create a cure for the Infection. They fight their way through zombie-infested towns and to find the "impregnable" CDC research station their hopes are pinned on.

YOLO! Not the Zombies! Book 3 Have you ever wondered how a hurricane might affect the zombie apocalypse? Or how undead would fare in a sandstorm? (Hint: Hope they aren't wearing a helmet.) These and other natural disasters are explored in these zombie short stories.

Forthcoming:

Survival Skills for All Ages: 26 Outdoor Life Skills covers basic camping skills such as knot tying, fire building, outdoor cooking, and choosing a tent. It also covers hunting, fishing, and foraging for food; finding your way using maps, compasses, and GPSs; and truly basic skills such as managing time and water safety (tides, currents, etc.).

Survival Skills for All Ages: Special Needs Prepping may sound like something for "other people" but most families have special needs: babies, the elderly, diabetes, asthma, allergies, even a simple sprained ankle or back injury can make us (temporarily) special needs.

Contact the Author

Bethanne Kim would love to hear from you! She maintains two blogs. The Moderate Mom focuses on politics. Wise Fathers avoids politics.

You can connect with her through:

Email–theWiseMom@WiseFathers.com

Blogs–TheModerateMom.com; WiseFathers.com

Facebook–The Moderate Mom; Wise Fathers

Pinterest–TheModerateMom; WiseFathers

Twitter–@TheModerateMom; @Wisefatherss

Amazon reviews really matter, especially for indie authors. Please take a few minutes and post a review of this book on Amazon.com.